With Faith Like Hers Bible Study Series

I am Esther

Carol Peterson, MTS

Honor Bound Books

Honor Bound Books

Interior typeset in 12/16/18pt Cambria, used with permission from Microsoft. Cover background by Viscious-Speed; used with permission from Pixabay.com.

ISBN: 9781951587109

Dedication

This book is written with thanks to my terrific husband, Jim who has supported each of my writing projects with unwavering loyalty, and who patiently supported me going to seminary to better prepare for and follow God's leading in my writing.

It is dedicated to the men and women today who have encouraged my faith, to the men and women recorded in Scripture who teach us still and to the God who loves us all.

CONTENTS

I am a Leader

I Know God is Good

Preface

It is human nature to explore who we are. It is part of the spiritual journey we take as Christians to explore who we are *in Christ* and seek to understand who God wants us to become. This women's Bible study series focuses on understanding ourselves as Christian women.

I grew up in a Protestant Christian home. My father was a pastor so naturally I sat in the pew every Sunday and listened to his sermons. We also visited other churches whenever we went on vacation, where I heard sermons from other pastors, too. One thing I began to notice very early was the number of sermons that focused on men in the Bible. They were men of faith and had valuable lessons for us to learn. But as a young girl, growing into an impressionable young woman, I wondered what I had in common with all those "old dead guys," as I thought of them.

When I began writing this series about women in the Bible, I found that other women felt the same way. The lives of these women had been recorded in our holy Bible. They were there for an important reason; written and instructed by the Holy Spirit to be included within the canon of the church. After reading one of my books in this series, a woman commented that she had always felt as if she was not as loved by God as men were. She knew that was not true at an intellectual level, but she had never gotten over that feeling, until she read one of my books in this series.

My goal with this series is to address that issue; to point out how dearly God loves women by pointing out how clearly God loved the women whose lives He instructed the men who wrote our Scripture and recorded those lives in our Bible. Moreover, I wrote this series with the idea in mind that "we women are part of God's ongoing plan, just as were those women in Scripture."

Scripture gives us examples of people who lived by faith. They were people just like us—with flaws and foibles; triumphs and turmoil. But they lived a victorious life because they lived in the light of God's love. Outward things have changed since biblical times, but people are basically the same. When we look at the lives of women in Scripture, we glimpse how God saw them. When we learn the lessons they learned, God can show us how He still sees His women today. We can say, "I am like her; I have her faith; I can survive her circumstances."

That is the basis of the *With Faith Like Hers* series. Each book takes the reader through 28 days of meditative Bible study. We look at a woman in Scripture and see how God—through His Word—viewed her and how He might view our lives in a similar manner. This book is Queen Esther's story. But it is also ours—when we have faith like hers.

The book you are holding is the second edition of *I am Esther*. Since writing the first edition, God instructed me to go back to school. "Really?" I asked God in surprise. "You do know that I am almost 70 years old," I asked. Silence. But in ultimate obedience to that call, I completed seminary. With my more secure understanding, I set out to revise this series of books. I was pleased (and more than relieved) to find that nothing in any of the books had been doctrinally incorrect. But I had more to say about each of these women. Sometimes a little; sometimes a lot. Thus, here is the new edition, complete with redesigned cover that include those power-packed initials after my name—MTS, referring to my Masters of Theological Studies. I add those little letters to give you one more speck of confidence that what I write is not something I whipped out of my back pocket. Contained in this book are lessons we can learn from Queen Esther, based on sound doctrine from mainstream Christianity, studied and prayed over to encourage you, my precious reader, to live your life *with faith like hers.*

Although this book is intended to be an individual daily study, it can also be used effectively as a group study. Simply divide each weekly discussion at the sections—discuss one section each week. Add day 1 in with the first week; add day 28 in with the final week. Some weeks will have fewer days than others, but none will require more than one reading per day.

For ease of reading, I have limited footnotes within the body of the book. Citations for many of the resources I used for research are listed in an "annotated" Bibliography. I have added a few to this newest edition, thanks to serious study in seminary. "Annotated" just means that each resource includes a brief description of the value that resource held for me in the research of this book. Those descriptions can help you in your personal research, should you like to pursue this woman more deeply.

I pray you will be blessed in your study of Queen Esther, and remember that your life—like hers—is part of God's ongoing plan.

A Note about Esther

The book of Esther in our Bible refers to the Queen both as Esther (her Persian name) and Hadassah (her Hebrew name). It refers to the King as both King Xerxes (as the Greeks knew him) and King Ahasuerus (his Persian name). In order to avoid confusion and simplify discussion during this study, I use the more commonly recognized and more easily pronounced names of Esther and Xerxes.

For the next 28 days, we will look specifically at the life of Queen Esther. Each lesson will explore one character trait or circumstance of Esther's life. Then we will examine: How can we live our lives like she did? How can our lives reflect what she has to teach us? How might God see us as His women of faith today in a way that reflects how He saw Queen Esther 4,000 years ago?

This is Esther's story. But when we learn the lessons taught us by this young Jewish woman from ages past, we can say, "I am like Esther. I understand her life. I can live my life like she did." We can remember that our lives, like hers, are a continuation of God's plan.

Day 1—Becoming Like Esther

I love the book of Esther. Growing up, I heard the Bible stories just like you did. I knew who Noah was; what was Moses' claim to fame. I could even name the 12 disciples. But what I just didn't get out of the characters preserved in Scripture was what all those old, dead men had to do with me—this wee little girl trying to figure out life in the modern world.

Then I spent a rainy, seventh grade lunchtime in the library where I found a book that changed my life. I don't remember the title or its author. All I remember was how much I loved it. I read it cover to cover, three times through. It was the story of a beautiful young woman; the winner of an ancient beauty contest, who became queen and saved her people.

Was I surprised when my mother told me it was based on a book of the Bible? You bet I was! For the first time in my little life, a character from the Bible came alive. I too was a young woman. I longed to be seen as beautiful; better yet, to be seen as the most beautiful young woman in the land. And to be courageous enough to save her people? Yes, I wanted to be like that, too.

Thus began an interest in other characters preserved in Scripture—even those old, dead men might have something to teach me, alive and lovely as I was. But it was the book of Esther that drew me back again and again to the Bible. Esther's haunting story of beauty, courage, power, and faith is timeless. Despite the fact that God is not even mentioned in the book.

He may not be mentioned by name, but God is definitely present throughout the book of Esther; just as He is present today everywhere we are. Over the years, God has called me to return to the book of Esther for what I might learn from that beautiful young woman who lived thousands of years ago in a far off land. The reading is richer, of course when we know more about the people, the history, and the society in which the events took place. So let's summarize a few key points before we move forward.

The Characters

Esther: Haddassah was Queen Esther's Hebrew name. Esther was the name she took or was given when she became Queen. Her parents had died, leaving her cousin Mordecai to look after her.

Xerxes was the Persian King. He was known to the Hebrews as Ahasuaras. His father was King Darius the first. His mother was Atossa, daughter of Cyrus the Great. It was Cyrus the Great who had conquered Babylon and allowed the Jews to return to Jerusalem. Although the Jews living in Persia at this time were still considered "exiles" from Israel, they remained there of their free will or due to economic, familial or hardship issues which meant they had not or were unable to return to their homeland.

Vashti was King Xerxes' first queen, deposed when she refused his summons. Although there is some disagreement about her lineage most scholars infer she was royalty in her own right, claiming that she was daughter and surviving heir of Belshazzar, the last Babylonian monarch, and thus also the great-great granddaughter of Nebuchadnezzar, whose dream was recorded in Daniel 2 and who destroyed the Temple.[1] If so, Vashti might have even considered herself to be the legitimate heir to the throne, rather than Xerxes.

Relationship between Haman and Mordecai. Mordecai was a Jew from the tribe of Benjamin (Esther 2:5), which is the tribe from whom King Saul, the first King of the Jews, descended.[2] When the Jews left Egypt with Moses, the first people who attacked them were the Amalekites (Exodus 17:8-16). God later ordered King Saul to destroy them, including their King Agag. After Saul disobeyed God and allowed King Agag to live, Samuel (who had anointed Saul) killed Agag himself, hacking him to pieces (1 Samuel 15). Haman, King Xerxes' highest official was a

---

[1] Calef, Susan and Ronald A. Simkins, ed., "Women, Gender, and Religion," *Journal of Religion & Society* Supplement Series 5 (2009), 166, citing *Panim Acherim* 56-60; *1* and *2 Targum Esther* 1.9; *Esther Rabbah*1.9, 10; see also Zucker, D. J. (2024). "Viewing Vashti: as Victim, as Vilified, and as Venerated." *Women in Judaism: A Multidisciplinary E-Journal*, 20:1(2024), 6.

[2] Eric Ortlund, Ian M Duguid., James M. Hamilton Jr., Jay Sklar, *ESV Expository Commentary, Vol. IV Ezra-Job* (Wheaton, IL: Crossway, 2020), 257.

descendant of King Agag. Thus, Mordecai and Haman hated each other based on family and cultural history.[3]

When in History

The events of the book of Esther took place during the height of power of the Persian Empire. The time was between 485-464 BC, about 100 years after Babylonian King Nebuchadnezzar II destroyed Jerusalem and took the Jews into captivity (Daniel's time).[4] The events are believed to have occurred about 50 years after King Cyrus freed the Jews to return to Israel and before Greek Alexander the Great conquered the Persian Empire.

The Books of the Old Testament are not presented in chronological order. Although the book of Esther is the seventeenth book of the Old Testament, only portions of the books of Ezra, Nehemiah, and Malachi contain Old Testament history later than Esther. Based on the historical reign of King Zerxes, there were somewhere between 464 and 485 years between the story of Esther and Jesus' birth.

The Society

The events in the book of Esther occurred in the capital city of the Persian Empire, the location of modern day Iran. Xerxes exercised absolute, complete control over people from a variety

---

[3] George Arthur Buttrick, *Interpreter's Bible; Vol. III* (New York: Abingdon Press, 1952), 841.

[4] Victor P. Hamilton, *Handbook on the Historical Books* (Grand Rapids, MI: Baker Academic, 2001), 504, 532.

of cultures. Both the Persian and Jewish societies were patriarchal. That meant unmarried women were the property of their fathers or the male head of house and could be married off for a bride price. Marriages were arranged by male family members, often before puberty. So Esther, a virgin, was probably quite young.

Esther would not have expected to have a say in her future. She would not have thought to defy her guardian or the empire. Her feelings of being taken into the harem would have been considered inconsequential when the book of Esther was written. She had no choice but to obey the King's command. Disobedience would have meant death for her and probably for Mordecai. However, Esther was able to skillfully use the power of a male-dominated world to accomplish something still celebrated annually more than 2500 years later.

Esther's Eternal Impact

We read the story of Esther and are impressed with her beauty, courage, and strength. She saved her people from annihilation. But what she did also had an eternal impact. Throughout the history of the Jewish people up until her time, the long-awaited Messiah was told that he would be born in the small town of Bethlehem in Judeah (Micah 5:2). That bit of prophecy was part of God's plan. During the time of Esther, Bethlehem was part of the great Persian Empire. The decree arranged by evil Haman allowed for the Jews to be slaughtered not only in the capital city of Suza. Jews would have been slaughtered throughout the empire—wiped from existence—even in the small town of Bethlehem. While God's plan could have been fulfilled in another way, it wasn't. The Messiah was born in Bethlehem, just as God, through the prophet said He would. God's plan moved forward smoothly and without a hitch, in no small way because He used Esther for His good purpose. He had put her in the right place at the right time so that she could be used by Him.

When I ventured into the writing of this book about Esther, God gave me a verse to help me focus on what we could learn.

> *And who knows but that you have come to royal position for such a time as this* (Esther 4:14).

When I mentioned this new "life verse," my brother chuckled, saying, "What? Now you're a queen?" Without a single thought of my own to rely on, the Holy Spirit filled my mouth with the proper response:

"No, but I'm the daughter of the King and He can use me right here and right now for His good purpose."

That Spirit-filled proclamation led me to understand what God wanted me to share: we modern gals can learn a lot from the character and circumstances of Esther. When we do, we get a glimpse of who we might be in God's eyes. Although this is Esther's story, it is also ours, when we have faith like hers. At that point, we can say

"I am like Esther."

Please read the book of Esther as we study together. It's just ten little chapters. Chapter 10 contains only three sentences. You can read it all in one sitting; but take your time and enjoy the glory and depth. We start tomorrow, digging in and digging deep.

For Thought and Discussion

- Have you had a tough time relating to men and women in Scripture? Who do you most relate to? Why?

- Is there one thing you most love about the story of Queen Esther? What is it? What might you not understand at this point?

- Do you have a life verse? Do you live it? How might you ask God to help you live Scripture better?

PRAYER: Heavenly Father, thank you for giving us Scripture to meditate on and learn from. Thank you for making me teachable, Jesus, and for not giving up on me as I sometimes stumble along in my faith. Show me how you see me as your precious daughter—daughter of the King. Amen.

My Circumstances

Day 2—I am an Orphan

Another of my favorite childhood books was Frances Hodgson Burnett's *The Secret Garden*. It is the story of Mary Lennox, a young orphaned girl sent to live with her uncle. It is also the story of her crippled cousin, a virtual orphan, having lost his mother physically during childbirth and his father emotionally at her death. I now watch the movie version several times a year, most recently last night—tissue in hand; soggy by the end.

I was blessed to have an intact, functional, Christian family. Both my mother and father loved me and were present, active parents. Yet I loved *The Secret Garden* and, at a soul level, I understood Mary Lenox, an orphan girl, heartsick for parental love.

The book of Esther describes the wealth and grandeur of King Xerxes' court along with the glamour of Esther's place in the palace. When we read the book of Esther though, we sometimes forget that Esther was an orphan, raised by her cousin, Mordecai.

> *Mordecai had a cousin named Hadassah, whom he had brought up because she had neither father nor mother* (Esther 2:7).

Mordecai tried to do what was best for Esther. He counseled her, trained her, and encouraged her heritage. But no one can take the place of a parent. Esther must have had a deep empty place in her heart because she had been left an orphan.

God's plan for our earthly lives is that children be cherished and raised by a loving father and mother. Scripture recognizes the emotional and physical needs of orphans, placing on our hearts as Christians, an extra level of care for them.

> *Religion that God our Father accepts as pure and faultless is this: to look after orphans and widows in their distress and to keep oneself from being polluted by the world* (James 1:27).

Throughout the Book of James, the reoccurring theme is that although we are saved by faith in Jesus Christ, our faith will bear fruit by what we do. And God sees our faith as pure and faultless when one thing we do is look after orphans and widows.

Many of us have been blessed with parents in our lives who cared for us as we matured into adulthood and beyond. But still, we often feel a separation between ourselves and our parents. When we were small children, we leaned on our parents for guidance in everything we said and did, modeling them as closely as we could. Yet often we felt as if we weren't quite getting it right; feeling as if we weren't "earning" their love.

As young adults, many of us went the opposite direction, vehemently believing that our parents knew nothing about what was good for us; what made us happy; how we wanted to live our lives. Even at a point when our values and those of our parents coincided, still there was a sense of separateness from them. We recognized that we had received life from them. We recognized the part they had played in our growth and development. We were grateful for the good things we became and forgiving in ways they had fallen short of the parenting we may have needed. But often there remained a feeling of separateness.

People raised without a loving father and mother know firsthand the loss and heartache of childhood.

God placed in our hearts not just a need for earthly parents who would steward our lives. He also placed in our hearts a deep need to be His children; to allow Him to be our eternal, Heavenly Father—the One who could provide our every need with no separation between us as we spend eternity in His arms. Psalms addressed this need.

> *Though my father and mother forsake me, the LORD will receive me* (Psalm 27:10).

Whether we have earthly parents; whether our earthly parents were good parents to us, we still need a spiritual father. Without God, we are spiritual orphans. Jesus confirmed this.

> *"If you love me, keep my commands. And I will ask the Father, and he will give you another advocate to help you and be with you forever—the Spirit of truth. The world cannot accept him, because it neither sees him nor knows him. But you know him, for he lives with you and will be in you.* ***I will not leave you as orphans****; I will come to you. Before long, the world will not see me anymore, but you will see me. Because I live, you also will live"* (John 14:15-21, emphasis added).

There are many kinds of love and many ways to love people. We love our husbands differently from the way we love our girlfriends. We love our children differently from the way we love any other person. We may not always like our children or agree with their choices, but we love them nonetheless. In a microcosm, that is how God loves us. He might not always approve of what we do or think or say or the choices we make, but He loves us anyway. In fact, he has always loved us anyway, to the point that He sent Jesus to provide the only blood sacrifice worthy of His forgiveness of those bad choices we make.

It is hard to conceptualize how God loves us spiritually. We understand His provision. We understand the way He may orchestrate events or circumstances. We even may understand a portion of His plan of salvation for us.

But in addition to the unconditional love God pours into our lives, He also unconditionally loves our souls. He recognizes that all of us have empty places in our hearts that only God can fill. Only the Holy Spirit, living in us, can parent us in the way our souls need. Only the love and forgiveness of Jesus can heal the wounds of spiritual childhood and grow us more like Him.

God recognizes that we are spiritual orphans in this world. He stands ready to adopt us into his family. Mordecai took over parenting Esther, as his own daughter. God will take over our spiritual parenting, when He adopts us into His family.

If Esther were here, she would say this was her story. She was an orphan and knew what it was to live without a father and mother who loved her unconditionally.

Who are we to God? When we recognize that we are spiritual orphans without our Heavenly Father, we understand how He might see His women of faith. We can answer:

I am like Esther.

For Thought and Discussion

- In what ways have you felt like an orphan—as a child, in school, at home, in society, at work, at church?

- Did you feel secure in your parents' love? Were there times you didn't live up to your parents' expectations?

- What does it mean to be a child of God?

PRAYER: Heavenly Father, thank you that I will never be orphaned, but am fully your child. Thank you, Jesus for making it so. Thank you, Holy Spirit for reminding me daily. Amen.

Day 3—I am an Exile in a Foreign Land

On my first major travel outside the US, my husband and I hit the capital cities of Europe. Five countries in eight days. You can imagine. Some days, we felt overwhelmed. So much to see. So much that felt alien and unknown. Outside of our sense of history. Different customs, different language, different food, smells, money. Different everything.

At one point, we had been walking through Vienna, Austria on our way from one notation on our map to the next. We stopped at a sidewalk café—the type of place where you walked inside, got your food and took it outside to sit at little tables along the street. It was lovely.

Of course, we didn't speak German and had no idea what the food was. But we had gotten used to pointing, raising the number of fingers to indicate what we wanted, and then holding out the strange looking bills and coins for the restaurateur to take what he required.

On this occasion, after several tries of pointing to the sausages we wanted from the glass case before us, we succeeded in making our purchase and settled down at a sunny table outside.

We opened our paper bag and retrieved—not the two sausages we thought we had ordered—but two slices of plain, dry bread.

No. We didn't go back and try ordering again. We humbly munched our bread and headed for a street side sausage cart where there was but one choice in the ordering. We had never felt so much like we had entered a foreign land than that day.

> *Now there was in the citadel of Susa a Jew of the tribe of Benjamin, named Mordecai son of Jair, the son of Shimei, the son of Kish, who* ***had been carried into exile*** *from Jerusalem by Nebuchadnezzar king of Babylon, among those taken captive with Jehoiachin king of Judah. Mordecai had a cousin named Hadassah, whom he had brought up because she had neither father nor mother* (Esther 2:5-7, emphasis added).

Scripture tells us that the Jews had been taken captive and carried into exile by King Nebuchadnezzar. The Jews living in Susa were away from their home. They were refugees, living in a foreign land among foreign people who had customs, language, and heritage that were different from their own. Although Cyrus the Great had allowed the Jews to legally return to Jerusalem (Ezra 1), many remained in Susa. It would have been a hardship to pick up and leave the life they had made in Susa. Nonetheless, the Jews living there, no doubt felt outcast, little more than slaves perhaps. They lived in a foreign land, at the hand of foreign kings, waiting for deliverance from God.

It is in this situation that the story of Esther plays out. She was part of a people in exile where there were fewer protective laws perhaps and where her status was less secure. Esther's cousin Mordecai warned her not to tell anyone that she was a Jewess—for her protection; so she would not be mistreated; so she would not be looked down on or despised.

> *Esther had not revealed her nationality and family background, because Mordecai had forbidden her to do so* (Esther 2:10).

In some situations, at some points in our lives—we too feel like we don't belong. We too feel as if we are in exile, in a foreign land, perhaps unprotected, mistreated, looked down upon, despised. Spiritually, Scripture tells us we are aliens in a foreign land until we turn to God.

> *...remember that at that time* [before Jesus] *you were separate from Christ, excluded from citizenship in Israel and foreigners to the covenants of the promise, without hope and without God in the world* (Ephesians 2:12, explanation added).

This verse indicates that those of us who were not Jewish to begin with—we Gentiles—were foreigners to the promises God had given to His chosen people, the Jews. If we had lived in Esther's time before Jesus, we non-Jews, non-chosen by God would have been exiled from His presence forever. Fortunately, because of Jesus, now

> *There is neither Jew nor Gentile, neither slave nor free, nor is there male and female, for you are all one in Christ Jesus* (Galatians 3:28).

In other words, once Jesus came and once He became the sacrifice for all people for all sins for all time, us non-Jews got to join God's chosen people and came out of spiritual exile, able to live forever with God's people.

> *Consequently, you are no longer foreigners and strangers, but fellow citizens with God's people and also members of his household* (Ephesians 2:19).

Paul furthers this thought, explaining our desire to live forever with God. Even the Jews of old, says Paul, knew they were looking for a heavenly country.

> *All these people were still living by faith when they died* [before Jesus' time]. *They did not receive the things promised them; they only saw them and welcomed them from a distance, admitting that* ***they were foreigners and strangers on earth****. People who say such things show that they are looking for a country of their own. If they had been thinking of the country they had left, they would have had opportunity to return.* ***Instead, they were longing for a better country—a heavenly one.*** *Therefore God is not ashamed to be called their God, for he has prepared a city for them* (Hebrews 11:13-16, emphasis and explanation added, see also Philippians 3:20-21).

God placed in our hearts a desire to be with Him; a desire to spend eternity in His presence; a need to return to the place of our true citizenship: heaven. This longing—unfulfilled here on Earth—makes us feel like we are exiled in a foreign land.

If Esther were here she would say this was her story. She was an exile, living in a foreign land.

Who are we to God? When we recognize that we are in exile from the presence of God until our eternal return to Him, we understand how He might see His women of faith. We can answer:

I am like Esther.

For Thought and Discussion

- Have you ever lived in a foreign country? What are some of the difficulties you might experience living outside your home country?

- How does being with people who don't share your customs, your language or religion make you feel about yourself?

- What does it mean that your true citizenship is in heaven? How does that affect the way you live your earthly life?

PRAYER: Heavenly Father, sometimes I feel like I don't belong. When I feel lost, please remind me that this is but a temporary home. Remind me that my true home is in heaven with you, Jesus and that you are waiting to welcome me home one day. Thank you, Holy Spirit for being with me each day until I return home to be with you. Amen.

Day 4—I Was Not Born Royal, But I Have Been Made Noble

ὦ

When I was nine years old, I started saving my money for something special. I had seen it one day while shopping with my mother at the department store. One glance and I knew I had to make it my own.

Nearly a year later, I returned with my mother, my black patent leather handbag clutched to my chest. I counted out my dollar bills and my quarters. Triumphantly I returned home with my long-desired treasure: a sparkling rhinestone tiara.

I made sure my daughter had her own rhinestone tiara before she turned ten. And—confession time—two years ago, I bought myself a brand new tiara, reliving the time when that sparkling piece of glass and metal had made me feel like a princess.

Esther was beautiful. She was also a queen. She probably had a tiara and no doubt it was dripping with jewels. But Esther didn't start out as royalty. Nor was the search that led her to the King intended to grant her nobility. The search was suggested by the King's servants and companions to find beautiful women to please the King.

> *"Let a search be made for beautiful young virgins for the king. Let the king appoint commissioners in every province of his realm to bring all these beautiful girls into the harem at the citadel of Susa. Let them be placed under the care of Hegai, the king's eunuch, who is in charge of the women; and let beauty treatments be given to them.* ***Then let the girl who pleases the king be queen instead of Vashti****"* (Esther 2:2-4, emphasis added).

Remember that many scholars believe Queen Vashti had been from noble birth, possibly she even felt as if she was the true heir to the throne, rather than her husband King Xerxes. If so, Queen Vashti was a noble. She had been born royal. King Xerxes' noble advisors suggested Queen Vashti be deposed "according to the law." (Esther 1:15). Think of the King's noble advisors as his Supreme Court Justices.

But it was not a group of legal advisors who came up with the idea for a new queen. It was the King's servants or companions who concocted that clever notion. Sure, let's bring in beautiful young virgins—lots of them—for the King's harem. And if one pleased the King, then—hey, here's an idea—let her be Queen.

The servants' idea was outside of legal thought. Nor did the servants suggest that young noble women be included in the search. Rather, they made a suggestion they thought would please the King; a way to bring him pleasure.

The search was for beautiful women from ordinary families in ordinary society; not for women of noble birth as would be fitting to become Queen of the Persian Empire. It is doubtful that any nobleman would allow his noble daughter to become part of a harem. A noble daughter's worth was in the political or financial power her marriage could bring to the family. That potential power would be wasted if she became a consort to the King; little more than a royal prostitute. No, the women heading to the King's harem were not likely of noble birth.

Still, at first reading it sounds like the stuff of fairytales. Not born into a royal family; but because of her loveliness, Esther was whisked off to the palace to live happily ever after. Princess Diana. Kate Middleton. Grace Kelly. Real-life fairy tales. The dreams of little girls. A desire to be Princess, Queen, Goddess. Set upon a throne. Loved by all.

But it doesn't happen that way in real life. Usually princesses are born princesses. Queens become queens through arranged marriages. There's that pesky thing known as "royal blood." Not that the blood is any different from a scientific point of view. But throughout history, royals have tried to maintain royalty—and power—by keeping royalty royal through heredity. Going back to the Egyptian pharaohs, the desire for royal purity meant that even brothers and sisters married to keep the lineage "pure."

That's one reason why the story of Esther is so intriguing. We don't know from Scripture what Queen Vashti's background was. But we do know that the King of Persia could have wed a royal woman and made her queen. Yet, he chose Esther. A woman of non-royal blood. An ordinary woman. A Jewess—her ancestors taken as captive slaves. She was made Queen of one of the greatest empires in history.

Esther was not a noble woman. She had no aspirations of power that might come from the possibility of becoming queen. Yet, once she was within the King's court; once the King himself made Esther his queen, he endowed Esther with nobility.

Servants and companions suggested the King find beautiful young virgins for his harem. The servants would not have particularly cared about a political marriage or the uniting of enemies through a royal wedding. Joining the harem however was not a voluntary process. Esther 2:8 tells us that the beauty contest was a result of the King's commandment and decree (or order and edict). The young women from throughout the kingdom "were gathered" and "were taken." By force, if necessary. Certainly without choice.

Would it have been an honor to be a member of the king's harem? It meant a life of luxury; possibly a better life for women who otherwise would have been forced to live in poverty. But being a member of the king's harem meant that marriage, traditional family, and freedom were no longer possible for those women. Surely marriage, family, and freedom—not dependent upon the whims of the king presently in power—would have been an important dream for women of that day. Just as it is today.

Thus Esther was taken to be part of the king's harem—an ordinary woman from an ordinary family in an ordinary part of society. Yet God used her for an extraordinary purpose to fulfill part of His extraordinary plan. Perhaps, as ordinary women in our modern world, God has a way to use us to fulfill His extraordinary plan, too. Are you willing to consider the possibility that the God of the universe could use you for His good purpose?

Most of us weren't born noble. Fortunately our worth in God's eyes is not dependent on whose earthly family we were born into. It does not matter to God who our parents were, because, when we accept Jesus' salvation, we are born again into His family. Although we were not noble born, we become nobility as children of God, adopted daughters and sisters.

> *In love he predestined us for* ***adoption*** *to sonship* [daughtership] *through Jesus Christ* (Ephesians 1:4-5, emphasis and explanation added).
>
> *See what great love the Father has lavished on us, that we should be called* ***children of God!*** (1 John 3:1, emphasis added; see also Romans 8:14-17, Galatians 3:25-27; John 1:12; 2 Corinthians 6:18).
>
> *For those God foreknew he also predestined to be conformed to the image of his Son, that he might be the firstborn among many* ***brothers and sisters*** (Romans 8:29, emphasis added; see also Hebrews 2:10-15).

Our Heavenly Father wants us to be one big, happy family. His adoption process began that first Christmas morning when Jesus temporarily set aside His own divine nobility in order to provide a way for our salvation. By accepting that salvation, Judge God signs the adoption papers that forever bring us into His eternal, noble family. We were not born noble, but we become a daughter of the King. Like Esther we are made noble.

If Esther were here she would say this was her story. She was not born royal, but was made noble.

Who are we to God? When we realize that although we were born ordinary, God has made us noble, we understand how He might see His women of faith. We can answer:

I am like Esther.

For Thought and Discussion

- How does a family's background affect an individual's ability to rise above circumstances?

- In what ways do you feel ordinary? In what way do you feel special?

- Is it difficult to call yourself a "daughter of the King"? Do you struggle with feelings of not being worthy of this title? How do you think Jesus sees you? How can you daily remind yourself that, as an adopted child of God, you are the daughter of the King?

PRAYER: Heavenly Father, thank you for loving me so much that you have adopted me as your daughter. It is such an honor to be your Princess—to be royalty in your eyes; to know that you are both King and Abba Father. Please help me understand the depth of your love that you would want to include me in your royal family. Please open my heart and mind to be used by you today. Amen.

Day 5—I am the Bride of the King

ᘛ⁐ᕐᐷ

My last name is Peterson. That's a Norwegian name. But with dark hair, dark eyes, and olive skin, I don't look Norwegian. Because the only part of me that is Norwegian is my name. I got that by marrying my blond, blue-eyed Norwegian-blooded husband.

Esther was born with a Jewish name: Hadassah. When she married the King of Persia, she got a new name—the Persian name, Esther. She also got a royal crown, a royal robe, and a royal life. She was not born into royalty but she married into it—when the King made her his bride.

> *Now the king was attracted to Esther more than to any of the other women, and she won his favor and approval more than any of the other virgins. So he set a royal crown on her head and made her queen instead of Vashti* (Esther 2:17).

We gain a lot of things through marriage. Like Esther, one thing we women gain is a new name. As a member of Christ's church, we become Christ's bride.

> *"Let us rejoice and be glad and give him glory! For the wedding of the Lamb has come, and his bride has made herself ready. Fine linen, bright and clean, was given her to wear." (Fine linen stands for the righteous acts of God's holy people.)* (Revelation 19:7-8).

Paul further explained this to the people in Corinth, saying,

> *I am jealous for you with a godly jealousy. I promised you to one husband, to Christ, so that I might present you as a pure virgin to him* (2 Corinthians 11:2).

When we receive Jesus, we marry into the family of Christ. The church, theologically, becomes the bride of the Lamb (Jesus). As His bride, we even take His name: Christ-ian. Cool how that works, isn't it?

This idea of the church as the bride of Christ is one of those pesky theologies that may (or may not even then) finally make sense when we're sitting at Jesus' feet up in heaven. I don't spend much time wondering how Christian men feel about being part of the community of faith that Jesus calls His "bride." But as for us women—what's not to love about the idea of being loved so much that we are joined forever with the One who loves us most?

The book of Ruth is universally acknowledged as a foretelling the coming of Jesus. Ruth (a Gentile) married into the literal, biological family of Jesus when her husband Boaz became her redeemer, just as Jesus became the redeemer for all of us through His sacrifice. The Book of Hosea similarly foretells the coming of Jesus as savior when God directed Hosea to marry an adulterous wife, symbolizing God's relationship to Israel, saying

> *I will betroth you to me forever; I will betroth you in righteousness and justice, in love and compassion. I*

> *will betroth you in faithfulness, and you will acknowledge the LORD* (Hosea 2:19-20).

In ancient Jewish marriage, the two people who were betrothed were then kept apart from each other for a time, generally a year or longer. During that time, they would each prepare for marriage. The woman would gather her household items. The groom would leave and return to his father's home to build a house for himself and his bride. Then the groom would return to his bride and take her with him to live in the house he built for them. Listen to what Jesus told His disciples before He returned to Heaven.

> *My Father's house has many rooms; if that were not so, would I have told you that I am going there to prepare a place for you? And if I go and prepare a place for you, I will come back and take you to be with me that you also may be where I am* (John 14: 1-3).

Jesus, our bridegroom promised Himself to us. Then He left us for a time, returning to His Father's house to prepare a place for us. During His time away, we are to remain faithful to Him and to do our part in preparing for our future as the Bride of Christ.

Coincidently, Scripture reinforces many of our modern-world traditions with the doctrine of Christ's bride. When we turn to Jesus, we are washed white as snow and when we go to heaven we get to wear white robes—gloriously beautiful; better than the most beautiful wedding gown found on Earth. It gives whole new meaning to the popular television show, *Say Yes to the Dress*.

A heavenly banquet will occur at our heavenly wedding too. There everyone can have their fill from the Tree of Life—better than the most luscious wedding cake ever baked on Earth.

Jesus will turn the living water into the most full-bodied champagne you've ever sipped. And, oh, the music! Can you imagine that first dance we'll have with our King as He sweeps us onto the dance floor and into His arms? Now that's a happily forever and ever after!

We saw yesterday that when we become a Christian, God adopts us into His family and we become nobility as a child of the King. As a member of Christ's church, we gain nobility a second way—through marriage as the bride of Christ. This is no arranged marriage. Jesus offered to share eternal life with us. Of our own free will and delight we enter the marriage with joy and excitement.

As a result, our nobility is assured on two counts. Not only are we adopted into God's family, but our noble status is confirmed a second way on the day of Christ through marriage, as the bride of the King. Not many of us were born noble by society's standards. But as Christians, we are the Bride of the King.

If Esther were here, she would say this was her story. She became the bride of the King.

Who are we to God? When we realize that, as part of Christ's Church, we are the beloved bride of the King, we understand how He might see His women of faith. We can answer:

I am like Esther.

For Thought and Discussion

- Do you have a married name that does not reflect your genetic heritage?

- If you are not married, how does the knowledge that you are the bride of Christ make you feel?

- If you had trouble yesterday understanding that you are noble because God adopted you into His family, how does conferring royalty through marriage encourage you?

PRAYER: Heavenly Father, thank you for loving me so much that you call me your bride. Thank you for loving me so much that you have assured my nobility in two ways. Help me remember my standing in your eyes and help me live up to the reputation you have given me as part of your royal family. Amen.

I am Beautiful to God

Day 6—I am Beautiful

ॐ

Remember my tiara? It made me feel beautiful. God has filled this world with beauty. And we are one of the most beautiful things He has created. God placed in a woman's heart the desire to be beautiful and for others to recognize that beauty. Sometimes we don't want to admit how much we crave being seen as beautiful. But it's okay. We ladies know we have that desire. We want to be beautiful and we want our beauty to be appreciated by others.

Men often say we women dress up for other women. We probably do. Let's face it: other women know how important it is to have our beauty appreciated. So who better to dress up for than someone who understands our need to be seen as beautiful and to have that beauty appreciated?

Think about the complimentary words we receive. Being called "pretty" is okay. Being called "cute" is almost demeaning. "Gorgeous" feels insincere. "Good-looking" makes us yawn. But when someone tells me I'm beautiful, I feel special, loved and lovely. Body and soul.

Dictionaries specify the differences. Pretty means to be attractive in a simple or delicate way. Cute usually implies a youthfulness. Good looking and gorgeous indicate a generally pleasing or attractive appearance. Being beautiful is more than all of these other adjectives. Being beautiful implies that one is aesthetically pleasing, excellent, and of a very high standard. I want God to look at me as excellent. I want to be held to His standard and not found lacking. I want to be beautiful to Him.

Esther 2:7 first introduces us to Esther.

> *Mordecai had a cousin named Hadassah, whom he had brought up because she had neither father nor mother. This girl, who was also known as Esther, was lovely in form and features.*

Esther was lovely in form and features. She was so beautiful she was taken to the King's palace as part of the harem—the plan devised by the King's servants to please their master. Immediately the eunuch in charge of the women was impressed with Esther and provided her with a beauty regime. She spent six month being treated with oil and myrrh and another six months with perfumes and cosmetics in preparation for her time with the King.

Esther was already beautiful but she got another whole year of beauty treatments. This beauty regime was for the King's benefit—to make the women in the harem even more beautiful and fragrant than they already were. But don't you think the women loved it, too? Wouldn't you love a year-long "spa" experience?

Jewish people traditionally were anointed with oil not just for beauty but in order to prepare them for power, strength, and honor and to make something holy. When King David was still a young man, he was anointed by Samuel (1 Samuel 10:1) in preparation for his taking the throne after Saul. David was anointed in preparation for the role of power and strength he would take on. Could God have been using Esther's beauty treatments to anoint her in preparation for the role He intended her to have in the salvation of His people?

Our bodies are a gift from God. Without our physical bodies, we cannot be His hands and feet in this world. If Esther hadn't been beautiful physically, she would not have been taken to live in the palace or been able to speak to the King in order to help her people. God gave Esther great physical beauty and then used that beauty to accomplish His purpose, to save His people from slaughter.

Our bodies are a precious gift. They are beautifully made. And no matter the state they are in because of age or illness or circumstance, they are beautiful, because they are God's and because they house the Holy Spirit that lives inside. We were created in God's own image (Genesis 1:27). There is nothing as beautiful as God Himself. Dwell on that a bit—we were made in the beautiful image of our beautiful God.

That said, God still desires more than outward beauty. He reminded Samuel that

> *People look at the outward appearance, but the LORD looks at the heart* (1 Samuel 16:7).

Throughout Scripture, we are reminded that it is the heart that is important to God and that a heart for God is a heart that is beautiful. Speaking to women specifically, God tells us

> *But more than physical beauty, God desires the beauty of a pure heart that loves Him. Your beauty should not come from outward adornment, such as elaborate hairstyles and the wearing of gold jewelry or fine clothes. Rather, it should be that of your inner*

self, the unfading beauty of a gentle and quiet spirit, which is of great worth in God's sight (1 Peter 3:3-4; see also Proverbs 31:30).

When we love God, obey His commandments, worship Him and seek His face, with a gentle and quiet spirit, the beauty of our hearts shines brightly. He sees and acknowledges our beauty. We are beautiful to Him. To King Jesus.

If Esther were here she would say this was her story. She was beautiful to her king.

Who are we to God? When we recognize that we are beautiful to God our King, we understand how God might see His women of faith. We can answer:

I am like Esther.

For Thought and Discussion

- In what ways do you feel beautiful? In what ways do you not?

- Growing up, did you have an ugly duckling complex? How did you grow into an acceptance of the beauty God gave you? In what ways do you still need to?

- How has your sense of being a beautiful creature created by a beautiful God changed since you met Jesus?

PRAYER: Heavenly Father, thank you for my life and for making me in your image. We know we are beautiful to you. Please help me see the beauty you gave me and recognize your beauty everywhere in this world. Amen.

Day 7—I Care for My Body

ஜ

When I was 29 it was easier for me to understand that God made me beautiful. The year I turned 60 I stopped calling myself "middle aged." It's not likely I'll live another 60 years here on this earth. I'm no longer in the "middle" of life; but am now firmly ensconced in the end part. In fact that's about the only thing that is firm any more. As my body sags and bags, I puzzle to understand how God still sees me as beautiful despite the crepe paper skin, drooping eyelids, and chicken wattle.

Despite all the signs of aging, I recognize that God made this body really well. Things still work—basically. I still walk and breathe and laugh and sing. And I'm still grateful every day that I can.

The book of Esther is silent on Esther's life after she helped God save her people. We have to use our imaginations to fill in the events of the rest of her life. Surely, she saw Mordecai more often; possibly even worked with him on ways to benefit the Jews or ensure their sense of community. As Queen, she no doubt lived out her life in luxury within the palace walls. Perhaps she had children; maybe even grandchildren. Perhaps her natural womanly desire for a family became a reality.

> *Before a young woman's turn came to go in to King Xerxes, she had to complete twelve months of beauty treatments prescribed for the women, six months with oil of myrrh and six with perfumes and cosmetics* (Esther 2:12).

Based on the year-long preparation Esther went through before she was first seen by the King, she likely continued to have her body taken care of throughout her life as queen. No doubt, Esther grew old gracefully. Her beauty likely matured over time; continuing to call out to others and gather them to her as a reflection of God's love; His beauty shining through her.

Are we able to grow old gracefully, too? Whatever physical shape we are in, we are responsible for our bodies. In Genesis God gave mankind stewardship over the entire world. But the very first thing He gave us personal stewardship over was our own bodies. We may have husbands and children and neighbors and friends we are responsible for taking care of. But first and last, God gave us stewardship over ourselves. He intends us to take care of ourselves as best we can—both physically and spiritually.

If we are not in our best shape physically, how can we effectively be His hands and feet in this world, accomplishing His purpose? If we are not in our best shape spiritually, how will we even know what His purpose is and how He can use us?

Esther spent one full year caring for her body to make it the best it could be for her King. Yes, she was young and firm at the time. Yes, she was more beautiful than most other women. But the point is that she took care of her body. And she did it for one purpose: to please the King.

Everything in heaven and earth belongs to God—the planets, the stars, the oceans and even us (Deuteronomy 10:14;

Psalm 50:10; Psalm 50:12; 1 Chronicles 29:11). He created us and we belong to Him. All of us. Even people who do not know Him still belong to Him. That doesn't just mean our souls. It means our physical bodies also. He has only given us responsibility for them while we are in this physical world.

> *Now it is required that those who have been given a trust must prove faithful* (1 Corinthians 4:2).

The responsibility over our bodies is a deep trust because our bodies are where the Holy Spirit—God Himself—resides.

> *Do you not know that your bodies are temples of the Holy Spirit, who is in you, whom you have received from God? You are not your own; you were bought at a price. Therefore* ***honor God with your bodies*** (1 Corinthians 6:19-20, emphasis added).

God gave each of us a body that is beautiful in His eyes. A body that can be used by Him. A body He meant for us to care for. These bodies are the hands and feet that God uses in this world to accomplish His plan and purpose; they are the tools that God has created. If we fail to care for our bodies, God's tools are not as strong or effective as they could be. The fault is not God's; it is ours when we fail to care for them the way we should.

Esther was treated with oil of myrrh for six months before she was presented to King Xerxes. Myrrh was used to consecrate and anoint people for power and to consecrate the Jewish priests to holy use. Have we allowed Jesus to anoint us for power and consecrate us to holy use by Him?

If Esther were here she would say this was her story. She knew the importance of caring for her body and knew that her beauty enabled her to accomplish God's purpose.

Who are we to God? When we recognize our duty to care for our bodies in a godly manner, we understand how He might see His women of faith. We can answer:

I am like Esther.

For Thought and Discussion

- Think about the miracles going on in your body. List as many as you can and thank God for each of them.

- How are you doing taking care of the body God gave you? What should you be doing that you're not? What should you stop doing?

- How might you be hindering God from using you to the fullest?

PRAYER: Heavenly Father, thank you for the body you have given me. I'm sorry when I don't appreciate it fully or take care of it the way you want me to. Please help me do a better job, Holy Spirit, and show me how you would like me to be your hands and feet in this world. Amen.

Day 8—I am Pure

ര※ൟ

Pure: *spotless; stainless; free from what weakens or pollutes; free from moral fault or guilt; marked by chastity*

God's plan for women is for us to be virgins until we are joined to one man in marriage. That's His wish because the Creator of the universe knows it is best for us. Unfortunately we sometimes think we know better than God. We desire to be loved by a man; we desire to please a man; we desire to be desired by a man. When we lack the patience to wait for God's plan or lack the emotional strength to say no, then in one weak moment we might abandon God's desire for our sexual purity. And then it is gone. Forever.

> *Now the king was attracted to Esther more than to any of the other women, and she won his favor and approval more than any of the other virgins* (Esther 2:17).

Esther was a virgin when we first meet her. She had never been with a man sexually. She was pure. If she had not been pure, she would not have been taken into the King's harem. She would not have been where she needed to be—inside the palace—in order to be used by God. Esther's purity was essential to God's plan.

Many women today despair over sexual impurity in their past. We cling to our past sin even after having given it to Jesus and having received his forgiveness. It's almost as if we cannot let it go; as if it's a reminder to us that once gone, we can never regain the purity given us by God. We wish we could have a do-over in that part of our lives. We wish we could have remained pure until marriage. We wish we could have honored purity in the way God does.

We ask for forgiveness. We repent. But the physical consequence has occurred. Our bodies are no longer sexually pure. Many women are not able to move on, feeling they have let down themselves, God, and their future husband whom God had prepared for them. We cannot change the past. We can only repent—turn away—and move forward on the new path as directed by the Holy Spirit.

We forget the power of God to renew; the power that He can make pure all things; can restore us to purity *in His sight*. Ultimately, it is not our sight that matters through eternity. It is His. If He sees our repentant selves as pure, who are we to disagree?

Moreover, although we cannot change our past physical impurity, we can—after receiving forgiveness—return to purity in spirit; washed, spotless, stainless, and free from guilt from that moment on.

Do unto others as you would have them do unto you is the Golden Rule, based on Jesus' scriptural truth of "love your neighbor as yourself" (Matthew 22:39; also Leviticus 19:18). Obviously, this relates to the way Jesus wants us to treat others.

But the Golden Rule works inwardly as well. I should treat myself with the purity that Jesus sees in the forgiven me.

When we give someone a reputation to live up to, they strive to live up to it. Tell someone they're a hard worker and they'll work harder. Tell someone they project confidence and they'll be more confident. Jesus sees the repentant you as pure. He has given you a reputation of purity to live up to. Accept that reputation and strive to live up to it. Try to live a life of purity. Because, more than just physical purity, God desires purity in our hearts. Jeremiah reminds us that:

> *The heart is deceitful above all things, And desperately wicked* (Jeremiah 17:9).

If our hearts are naturally deceitful and wicked and filled with filth and sin based on our human nature (they are), then how can we possibly hope for a pure heart? We can't. At least, not by anything we do on our own. Fortunately, there is one who has the power we lack. God.

> *Moreover, I will give you a new heart and put a new spirit within you; and I will remove the heart of stone and give you a heart of flesh. And I will put My Spirit within you* (Ezekiel 36:26-27).

God can clean us when we surrender ourselves to Jesus and put our trust in Him. God will then give us a new nature. When we become His new creation, the Holy Spirit comes into our hearts, resides there, and can begin the work to make and keep us pure. Yes, it's a constant struggle between the divine work of the Spirit and our human nature, but when we surrender to that work (each day, each moment, each breath), then God is creating in us the pure heart he desires and changing us into the women He had planned since the beginning of time. God has to do the part of purifying our heart when we surrender to Him. After that, our part is to continue God's work by not hindering what He is doing.

> *Finally, brothers and sisters, whatever is true, whatever is noble, whatever is right, whatever is pure, whatever is lovely, whatever is admirable—if anything is excellent or praiseworthy—think about such things* (Philippians 4:8).

Scripture is filled with encouragement to stay the path, to fight against humanity's natural tendencies toward what is impure and evil. God knows it's hard; but He wants what is best for us. What is best for us is to continue to work toward living a life that pleases Him. Here are a few more verses of encouragement:

- Psalm 51:10 *Create in me a pure heart, O God, and renew a steadfast spirit within me.*
- Psalm 73:1 *Surely God is good to Israel, to those who are pure in heart.*
- Psalm 119:0 *How can a young person stay on the path of purity? By living according to your word.*
- 1 Timothy 4:12 *Don't let anyone look down on you because you are young, but set an example for the believers in speech, in conduct, in love, in faith and in purity.*
- 1 Timothy 5:22 *Do not be hasty in the laying on of hands, and do not share in the sins of others. Keep yourself pure.*
- Philippians 1:9-11 *And this is my prayer: that your love may abound more and more in knowledge and depth of insight, so that you may be able to discern what is best and may be pure and blameless for the day of Christ, filled with the fruit of righteousness that comes through Jesus Christ—to the glory and praise of God.*

- 1 Peter 15-16 *But just as he who called you is holy, so be holy in all you do; for it is written: "Be holy, because I am holy."*
- Leviticus 20:7 *Consecrate yourselves and be holy, because I am the LORD your God.*
- Titus 2:14 *(Jesus) who gave himself for us to redeem us from all wickedness and to purify for himself a people that are his very own, eager to do what is good* (explanation added)

God's plan is to make us like Jesus. His purpose is nothing less than that we be pure in heart, just like Jesus. Jesus spoke to the issue of purity in the Beatitudes when He said: *"Blessed are the pure in heart, for they shall see God"* (Matthew 5:8).

It is the heart that God looks at. It is the heart that God can make pure and we can then work at keeping pure through our daily dependence upon Jesus' strength and the ongoing work of the Holy Spirit. We can focus on purity of heart even if our bodies are no longer physically pure. A pure heart will bring us closer to God. Close enough, perhaps, to see a tiny glimpse of His glory.

If Esther were here she would say this was her story. Because of her purity, she was in the right place to be used by God.

Who are we to God? When we recognize that God has created in us a pure heart, we understand how He sees His women of faith. We can answer:

I am like Esther.

For Thought and Discussion

- In what ways have you struggled with purity? In your past? Now?

- Have you asked for forgiveness for impurity in your past? Have you truly felt forgiven or do you cling to your impurity?

- How can you regain your sense of purity through thoughts and actions?

PRAYER: Heavenly Father, I acknowledge impurity in my life. I sometimes struggle to let go of my impurity even after asking your forgiveness. Please remind me today that I have been washed clean by your blood, Jesus. Help me see myself as you see me—forgiven and clean. Amen.

Day 9—I am Obedient

ᘛ⁐ᕐᘚ

One of the most loved Scriptures of all time is Psalm 23:

The LORD is my shepherd, I lack nothing.
He makes me lie down in green pastures,
he leads me beside quiet waters,
he refreshes my soul.
He guides me along the right paths
for his name's sake.
Even though I walk
through the darkest valley,
I will fear no evil,
for you are with me;
your rod and your staff,
they comfort me.

Jesus as my shepherd. Me as a little lamb. It's such a peaceful image. So filled with harmony and contentment. Can't you just picture Jesus holding His staff, walking along side you, keeping you on His path?

How does a shepherd herd his sheep? That staff he carries isn't just a handy walking stick. A shepherd uses it to guide the sheep in the direction he wants them to go. Think about the old phrase: Spare the rod and spoil the child. The rod and the staff are used by the shepherd to guide the sheep. By using the rod and the staff, the sheep obey the shepherd.

And the sheep are comforted. They trust the shepherd to guide them on the safe path—away from rocky cliffs and hungry beasts. Their obedience to the good shepherd is comforting because they know that obedience is for their good.

Good parents make good rules. Good children obey those rules and do well. Bad parents make poor rules or make no rules at all. Without rules, children have nothing to obey. The result is usually poor choices and poor lives. Underneath the whining and attempt at rebellion, children need rules. At some level they understand that good parents care enough about them to make and enforce rules. Obedience is a reflection of a loving parent/child relationship.

> *But Esther had kept secret her family background and nationality just a Mordecai had told her to do, for she continued to follow Mordecai's instructions as she had done when he was bringing her up* (Esther 2:20).

Esther was a good girl. She did what she was told to do by those in authority over her. Would Esther have been selected for the harem had people known she was a Jewess? Possibly. The point though is that she was obedient to her cousin, followed his counsel and as a result was in the proper place to be used by God to save His people.

Later, as queen, Esther was obedient to her husband the King. He had authority over her not just as her husband but also as her king. It was his authority as king that caused her to fear what Mordecai asked her to do—go before the King to plead on behalf of her people. If she sought audience with the King without being summoned, the King had the authority to have her put to death instantly. No pleading. No wait a minute, honey. No court trial with a jury of young Jewish women. And with the history of King Xerxes' banishment of the former Queen Vashti fresh in her memory, Esther surely wondered how secure her position was.

Esther accepted her role however, and approached the King, accepting his authority over her, saying that "if I die, I die." She was willing to be obedient, even unto death. Like Jesus was obedient to Father God.

Am I obedient to those in authority over me? Am I obedient to God—the ultimate authority in my life? When the King asks us to do something, are we obedient—without question? Without hesitation?

King Solomon was known as the wisest man in history, as evidenced by the Book of Proverbs, attributed mainly to him. At the end of his lengthy treatise in Ecclesiastes, he determined:

> *Now all has been heard; here is the conclusion of the matter: Fear God and keep his commandments, for this is the duty of all mankind* (Ecclesiastes 12:13).

Obedience is not a bad thing. In reality, if rules have been created for our good, then being obedient to those rules is the very best, smartest, and most awesome thing we can do. Being obedient is a really good thing! Culture today has celebrated the anti-hero. We applaud movies where the bank robber or misunderstood murderer is the main character we root for. We praise people who walk to the "beat of a different drummer." We sing Frank's song about "Doing it My Way" as if my way is the best way.

Most often, my way isn't the best way. But always, every time, forever and completely, God's way is the best way. He is our forever hero.

Want a few more verses about the joy and benefit of obedience to God? Here are a few:

> *If you love me, keep my commands* (John 14:15).
>
> *As obedient children, do not conform to the evil desires you had when you lived in ignorance* (1 Peter 1:14).
>
> *In fact, this is love for God: to keep his commands. And **his commands are not burdensome*** (1 John 5:3, emphasis added).
>
> *I have chosen the way of faithfulness (my free will; my choice; making your way my way); I have set my heart on your laws* (explanation added, Psalm 119:30).
>
> *Why do you call me, 'Lord, Lord,' and do not do what I say?* (Luke 6:46)
>
> *Very truly I tell you, whoever obeys my word will never see death"* (John 8:51).
>
> *But I gave them this command: Obey me, and I will be your God and you will be my people. **Walk in obedience to all I command you, that it may go well with you*** (God's way is the good way) (Jeremiah 7:23; explanation and emphasis added).
>
> See also Joshua 22:5; James 1:22-25; Titus 3:1; 1 John 2:17, Romans 6:17, John 14:21-23.

Obedience doesn't require low esteem; it isn't demeaning; it doesn't mean we are weak. In fact, obedience to God strengthens our faith and allows us to rely even more on the power of Jesus available to those who love Him. Esther submitted to God and to her king but continued to be strong and decisive. She was obedient and as a result, both her husband, the King and God honored her.

If Esther were here she would say this was her story. Because of her obedience she was able to save her people.

Who are we to God? When we recognize the power found in obedience, we understand how He might see His women of faith. We can answer:

I am like Esther.

For Thought and Discussion

- As an adult, how do you see your parents' rules differently than you did as a child?

- Who has authority over you today? How does that authority make you feel secure? I what ways do you want to rebel against that authority?

- Do you listen for God's guidance? Is there something you feel God is asking you to do? What one step can you take toward being obedient today?

PRAYER: Heavenly Father, help me be obedient to those in authority while maintaining my personal strength and integrity. Help me especially be obedient to you and show me what you desire for my life. Amen.

Day 10—I Seek God's Guidance

One of the very first times I *knew* God was answering my prayers had to do with me giving up control to Him. My husband and I had entered the time of parenting teens—when they are stretching, pulling back, and trying to find their way in independence. Old forms of parenting no longer worked. Offered rewards. Warnings. Threats. It all becomes a new world when the age digits move past a dozen.

One of our children was struggling with the nuances of high school; the independence accorded those students by the teachers; the higher expectations of self-motivation. My child was lagging farther and farther behind, dragging through the day, unable to figure out how to catch up.

It wasn't a crisis. There was no physical or mental danger involved. But it was a stress that I felt uniquely incapable of understanding or knowing how to handle. After weeks of angry nagging, feelings of incapacity as a parent, and more than a few tears, one dark night, I simply gave it all to God. I acknowledged that I had no idea what to do. I released it; lay the issue at Jesus' feet, and asked that He carry the burden.

The next morning, my child was up, dressed and ready for school before I was even out of bed. Could this be my teen? The one I had to drag from bed each morning? I knew then God had heard my prayer and that my husband and I were not parenting our children alone. I was simply to love my children with Jesus as the focus of our lives. I learned the importance of seeking God's guidance.

> *Go, gather together all the Jews who are in Susa, and fast for me. Do not eat or drink for three days, night or day. I and my maids will fast as you do. When this is done, I will go to the king* (Esther 4:16).

Although this verse does not say that prayer was involved, most scholarly commentaries indicate that the fasting done by Esther, her maids, and her community of believers was accompanied by prayer.[5] Prayer was not mentioned because back then fasting was nearly universally accompanied by prayer. There was no fasting without prayer; no reason to fast unless you were seeking God's guidance, power or presence.

There are two types of people when it comes to worry and food. There's that group (generally thin people) who lose their appetite when they're worried. The idea of food makes them feel sick. So they basically don't eat until the object of worry has been resolved.

Then there is the rest of the world which I'm part of. We eat everything in and out of sight when we're worried. It's not a matter of hunger. It's not even a matter of appetite. It's a matter of the physical comfort certain foods give us; the energy food provides; the activity it requires to keep our hands and teeth busy while we wait for the object of worry to resolve.

---

[5] Edith Deen, *All of the Women of the Bible* (San Francisco: Harper Collins, 1983), 148.

But take a look at Scripture and how often fasting and prayer are linked. The cool thing about fasting and prayer even for those of us with "hands-on eating compulsion" is that they are linked in a good way. Giving up food causes you to think about food even more. Although that sounds problematic, in reality it means that our attention is thus all perfectly focused in a tidy packet which is then easier to refocus on God. With that tidy packet of focus, you can spend more time in prayer—seeking God's will.

Scripture is filled with examples of people who fasted. Sometimes it was for specific occasions (2 Samuel 12:16) or holy days. Sometimes it was for safety (Ezra 8:21) or power (Acts 13:3). Sometimes it was an act of repentance (1 Samuel 7:6) or for mourning (2 Samuel 1:12) or before making decisions (Acts 13:2-3; 14:23). And it did not always involve fasting from food (1 Corinthians 7:3-5).

Are we guided by prayer? Do we recognize our need for God's help? Are we asking for and giving prayer and guidance to others? And while we are praying (and fasting), are we doing it for our personal sense or in order to spend time with our Lord?

> *And when you fast, do not look gloomy like the hypocrites, for they disfigure their faces that their fasting may be seen by others. Truly, I say to you, they have received their reward. But when you fast, anoint your head and wash your face, that your fasting may not be seen by others but by your Father who is in secret. And your Father who sees in secret will reward you* (Matthew 6:16-18).

Remind you of another verse about praying in secret? Going into a closet to spend time alone with Jesus? (Matthew 6:6) Not for what others will say about our righteousness, but so that God will be able to look into our hearts and so that we will be able to hear His voice more clearly. More reason not to look gloomy. God desires our presence with Him. He desires us to seek us and when we do, He's right there—in the closet with us. Not in the dark, but with His light shining brightly into and through us.

If Esther were here she would say this was her story. She knew the importance of seeking God's guidance.

Who are we to God? When we recognize that God desires us to seek His guidance, we understand how He might see His women of faith. We can answer:

I am like Esther.

For Thought and Discussion

- How do you seek guidance from God? Through prayer? Scripture? Teachings by others?

- Have you tried fasting and prayer? If so, what was your experience?

- If you have not tried fasting and prayer, might you consider giving up an activity or a food or all food for a period of time in order to be able to focus more on God?

PRAYER: Heavenly Father, thank you for your guidance. I recognize that I can't do life on my own. I need you to show me your way. Help me find more ways to seek your guidance. Amen.

My Relationship with God

Day 11—God Can Use Me Wherever I Am

ᘛᘚ

My husband is an adventurer. Wherever he is, it's a place to explore. Often, that means he ends up in places he shouldn't; such as when he went on a sightseeing trip in Israel and ended up in the demilitarized zone surrounded by machine gun fire. On the other hand, sometimes hubby is in exactly the right place, such as when he sat next to the director of a Christian mission on an airplane and began a multi-decade relationship with him of helping spread Jesus' love across the globe.

Being in the right place might include simply holding the hand of someone I meet at the hospital and praying for their encouragement. Or being the one to give a smile or word of cheer to a person at the grocery store, when the only sense they have has been discouragement or despair.

> *For if you remain silent at this time, relief and deliverance for the Jews will arise from another place, but you and your father's family will perish. And who knows but that you have come to royal position for such a time as this?* (Esther 4: 14)

Esther was living in luxury. Esther was safe within the palace walls. Esther was Queen. If she had kept silent, *maybe* no one would have known she was Jewish. *Maybe* she would have been spared. Or maybe she and her family would have perished as Mordecai suggested.

But that didn't happen. Even though Esther was safely ensconced within the palace walls, God still used her. In fact, God used her *because* she was within those palace walls—right there where He put her in preparation to carry out His plan and be used by Him.

Sometimes God calls us to *go* for him, as He did with Samuel.

> *Then I heard the voice of the Lord saying, "Whom shall I send? And who will go for us?"*
>
> *And I said, "Here am I. Send me!"* (Isaiah 6:8)

Notice what Samuel said. "Here am I." Samuel was right there where God could find him—ready and willing to go for the Lord. Are we willing to go? Are we willing to stay? Are we willing to let God use us wherever we are?

God places each of us in situations. Is it chance that we are right here, right now? Has God perhaps specifically placed us where we are for His purpose? Or can He at least use us wherever we are? Of course He can.

God *can* use someone else. In fact, God can do whatever He wants Himself without any human help at all. But we are right here. Why *wouldn't* God use us? Esther realized the possibility that God placed her in her position for His purpose. She willingly allowed Him to use her.

Have you ever sat in church listening to a sermon and wondered whether the Pastor had been lurking outside your window watching your life? Have you wondered how he knew exactly what you needed to hear that Sunday morning? Do you suppose God orchestrated the Pastor's sermon and your attendance that Sunday so that you were in the right place to hear the message you needed to hear?

If God could create the universe by speaking words, certainly He could make sure you were where you needed to be to hear what you needed to hear. Or to make sure the Pastor was in the right place to preach the words others needed to hear.

If Esther were here she would say this was her story. God used her right where she was.

Who are we to God? When we realize that God can use us right here where we are, we understand how He might see His women of faith. We can answer:

I am like Esther.

For Thought and Discussion

- Have you ever clearly been in the wrong place at the wrong time? Describe what happened. What did you learn from the experience?

- Have you ever clearly been in the right place at the right time? Describe what happened. What did you learn from the experience?

- How does Esther's example help you think differently about being used wherever you are?

PRAYER: Heavenly Father, I know you can do all things. I acknowledge however that you want me to be your hands and feet in this world and help you accomplish your plan. Help me remember that your Spirit is right here inside me empowering me to do your will. Remind me that right here where I am is part of your mission field. Amen.

Day 12—God Can Use Me Right Now

One of these days . . .Just wait until . . .I'll get around to it when . . .

Are you a procrastinator? I'm generally not. I like to create a plan, set up a step-by-step guide on how to accomplish it and then start off. But sometimes, I'll be working that plan and reach a point when it looks like I'll have to move on to that final step—making it work.

When husband and I were designing and building houses, I'd invariably get to that point while I was drafting the plan. I was fine purchasing the property. The floor plan, foundation plan, roofing plan, electrical, plumbing, and window details all looked great. But once I got to the point where it needed to go to the building department for approval, I panicked. Ultimately I was going to have to start actual construction. That plan—so nicely detailed—was going to get built.

That's when fear set in. What if the actual house looked goofy? What if it was so bad we couldn't sell it? Worse, what if the building department refused to grant a permit or if they did, the design was faulty and the whole thing collapsed? Yes, a creative mind can think up all sorts of horror stories. Fear can cause you to stop forward movement or stop you before you even get started.

I so desire to be used by God. But sometimes I wonder if I'm up to what He has in mind. I'm just little me, after all. And He's great big God! I forget that God uses all sorts of people to accomplish His plan. Those people in the Bible weren't perfect either. But God used them anyway, right where He needed to use them. And right when He needed them. I'm not perfect. But fortunately I don't have to be perfect to be used right here and right now by God. He, after all, *is* perfect!

> *For if you remain silent at this time, relief and deliverance for the Jews will arise from another place, but you and your father's family will perish. And who knows but that you have come to royal position* ***for such a time as this****?* (Esther 4: 14, emphasis added)

Let's take the lesson we learned yesterday one step further: maybe God has placed us right here where we are or maybe we've wandered to this place on our own. Regardless, here we are. And God can use us where we are *right now*—for such a time as this.

Ephesians reminds us of good time management:

> *Be very careful, then, how you live—not as unwise but as wise, making the most of every opportunity* [some versions say *making the best use of the time*], *because the days are evil. Therefore do not be foolish, but understand what the Lord's will is* (Ephesians 5:15-17, explanation added).

God has plans for our lives and part of those plans include us helping Him work those plans. God has given us specific talents and abilities. He has given us time and has placed people and circumstances in our lives. He desires us to use those talents, abilities, time, and circumstances for Him.

> *For we are his workmanship, created in Christ Jesus for good works, which God prepared beforehand, that we should walk in them* (Ephesians 2:10).

Are we ready to be used by God? Are we available? Are we ready to be used by God *now*? Are we open to the possibility? Or are we waiting for a day in the future; a "one of these days" period in time that is us getting around to it? Do we really want God to look at our hearts and know that we only want to join God's team when we have nothing better to do?

If Esther were here she would say this was her story. God was able to use her right then.

Who are we to God? When we realize that God can use us right now, this very moment—and become willing participants—we understand how He might see His women of faith. We can answer:

I am like Esther.

For Thought and Discussion

- Have you felt God leading you to do something for Him but argued that the time wasn't right? How much of your argument might be fear or uncertainty rather than timing?

- Have you ever used the excuse that "someone else could do it better than I can"? Did someone else ultimately step up and do it? Did you feel a sense of relief or feel you had let God down? How might you have felt if you had been obedient right when you sensed God's leading?

- What area of your life might God be trying to use you right here and right now? How can you step out in faith and follow His leading?

PRAYER: Heavenly Father, I want to be used by you. I'm not always aware of how you might use me though. Please help me attune my heart and mind to the leading of your Spirit in me. Please show me ways that you want to use me right here and right now where I am. Amen.

Day 13—I Use My Power Wisely

ര്

In the movie, *Bruce Almighty*, Jim Carrey's character thought he could do a better job at managing the universe than God. So God gave him temporary power. The first thing Bruce did was rearrange the heavens, pulling the moon closer to the earth, causing tidal waves and destruction. The next thing he did was answer everyone's prayer requests with "yes," causing riots in the streets and general world-wide chaos. Ultimately Bruce learned that only God is able to wield ultimate power wisely. We laugh at the movie and Bruce Nolan's frivolous use of power. But how many of us would do any better? Wouldn't all of us love to grant everyone's heart-felt prayer request with a gracious "yes"?

Esther went from being a young innocent girl to being the queen of the largest kingdom at that time in history. She knew her new position came with power; yet she used that power wisely. When it became apparent that she needed to intercede on behalf of her people, she didn't stomp her foot and demand the King's action. Rather, she moved slowly. She sought her cousin's advice. She fasted. She sought God's guidance and then she approached the King with humility.

Can we understand the reality of Esther's situation? As the queen of the Persian Empire, she held the potential power to speak with the King face-to-face on behalf of her people. That's power!

Even though King Xerxes invited Esther into the inner court and said that whatever her request was, it would be granted, Esther still used her fledgling power wisely. She invited the King and his official to lunch. There King Xerxes asked for her request, indicating it would be granted. But once again, she simply requested the King and his official to dine with her one more time. By the second banquet, the King understood that her request was not trivial but something of deep importance to Esther. It was at that second banquet, that Esther then humbled herself before the King, falling at his feet. After telling him she and her people were to be slain, she left the matter to the King to address.

We hold power through Jesus. We have been *em*powered by Him to do His work.

> *So Christ himself gave the apostles, the prophets, the evangelists, the pastors and teachers, to equip his people for works of service, so that the body of Christ may be built up* (Ephesians 4:11-12).

Scripture also encourages us to be wise. There's a whole book (Proverbs) that contains nothing but thoughts about wisdom. Knowledge and wisdom are compared to rare jewels and treasures (Proverbs 8:11, Proverbs 16:16; Proverbs 3:14-15; Proverbs 20:15; Proverbs 2:4, to name a few). And God wants us to gain wisdom by receiving it from Him.

> *For the Lord gives wisdom; from his mouth comes knowledge and understanding* (Proverbs 2:6)

Job nicely combines the two issues of wisdom and power succinctly, saying

> *Wisdom is with the aged, and understanding in length of days. "**With God are wisdom and might**; he has counsel and understanding* (Job 12:12-13, emphasis added)

Wisdom and might. With God you get both.

Fortunately, no longer must our requests and concerns be presented to God through a human priestly representative. We have the power to go directly to Jesus. But that power comes with the need for wisdom. He invites us to bring our requests to him. Then we too, need to fall at Jesus' feet and leave them for Him to address. Esther shows us that we should present our requests with humility; relying on the King's will and justice. That is wise and it is powerful.

Esther made her request humbly. She asked for her own life and that of her people. In fact, she divided her request into two. Her *wish* ("petition" in the NIV) was for herself and her *request* was for her people. She therefore tied her own fate to that of the Jews. Basically, she asked for her own life, which would have been shocking to the king.[6] The life of his queen, his wife, safely ensconced within the walls of the palace, in danger? Moreover, Xerxes was not only shocked, he was angry (Esther 7:7). In short, Esther's humble plea had shocked and angered her husband the king. He was prepared to act.

If Esther were here she would say this was her story. She knew she had power but she used it wisely.

---

[6] Ortlund, *ESV Expository Commentary*, 277.

Who are we to God? When we recognize the power we hold through Jesus and seek His will, we understand how He might see His women of faith. We can answer:

I am like Esther.

For Thought and Discussion

- Describe a time when you felt powerful. Why did you feel that way? Was the power given you by someone else? Or were you empowered from within?

- Describe a time when you felt helpless due to power or authority over you. Was that power deserved or misused?

- Have you ever felt empowered by Jesus in a way that was outside your own doing? How might that experience empower you in the future? How might you use that experience as a personal testimony of your faith to others?

PRAYER: Heavenly Father, I sometimes feel helpless. Other times I recognize that I have power but don't know how to use it wisely. Please remind me that I can do all things through you because you strengthen me and give me power through your Holy Spirit living in me. Please grant me wisdom to use this power wisely for your glory. Amen.

Day 14—I am Steadfast

I'm a turtle. Metaphorically speaking. I'm one of those folks who live the saying, "slow and steady wins the race." Just like the turtle won the race over the speedy rabbit, it sometimes takes me a while to get myself going in the right direction or establish the right gait or the right attitude. But once I've set myself on the track, I just keep plodding along toward the goal. I think God likes that quality in me.

My husband gets brilliant ideas and sets us all on the highway toward the goal. But his struggle is to keep on the highway when he gets distracted by the interesting scenes along the way. That's also a godly quality because he's always seeing the potential, the need, the solution. He's steadfast in his ability to continually see new needs and how to address them. We make a good team—Jim gets me going and I drag him along to the finish. Between the two of us, we can keep on Paul's race we're running for Jesus.

Scripture doesn't indicate that Esther was a runner or that she did any type of cardio exercise at all. But if she had been a runner, she would have been a long-distance runner. In it for the long haul. Because she was steadfast.

> *Mordecai had a cousin named Hadassah, whom he had brought up because she had neither father nor mother. This girl, who was also known as Esther, was lovely in form and features* (Esther 2:7).

Esther had two names. Historians speculate that her Jewish name, Hadassah was given to her at birth and that she was given the Persian name, Esther when she entered the palace. Hadassah means "myrtle" and implies steadiness; steadfastness. Esther means "star"[7] and reflects her brilliant beauty as queen.

Despite the meaning of the name Esther, her nature was not that of a bright flash of brilliance that faded with her new-found glory. Rather, Esther's true nature is reflected in her original Jewish name. Throughout the book of Esther, she shows her steadfast nature. She obeyed her cousin. She obeyed the Eunuch Hegai. She obeyed God. She proceeded in all things with resolve, dedication, persistence, consistency, unwavering faith, and commitment. And because of her steadfast nature, Esther shone. Her physical beauty was enhanced by her inner, firm, and unwavering nature.

Paul reminds us to be steadfast.

> *Therefore, my dear brothers and sisters, stand firm. Let nothing move you. Always give yourselves fully to the work of the Lord, because you know that your labor in the Lord is not in vain* (1 Corinthians 15:58).

But Esther was also like her Persian name. She shone; not like a shooting star that flew across the sky and then was

---

[7] Ibid., 257.

extinguished. Rather, she shone like a star, lighting the sky in a steady, steadfast manner, reminding us of something the Apostle Paul encourages us to do:

> *Do everything without grumbling or arguing, so that you may become blameless and pure, "children of God without fault in a warped and crooked generation."* ***Then you will shine among them like stars in the sky as you hold firmly to the word of life.*** (Philippians 2:15-16, emphasis added).

What is our nature? Are we steadfast? Are we dedicated, persistent, consistent, committed, unwavering? In the race of faith we run, are we sprinters? Or, like Paul and Esther, are we long-distance, endurance runners? And while we're running, are we shining brightly, filled with the light that comes from Jesus?

If Esther were here she would say this was her story. She was steadfast, committed and unwavering.

Who are we to God? When we recognize the importance of being steadfast and seek to live that characteristic, we understand how God might see His women of faith. We can answer:

I am like Esther.

For Thought and Discussion

- In what areas of your life are you steadfast?

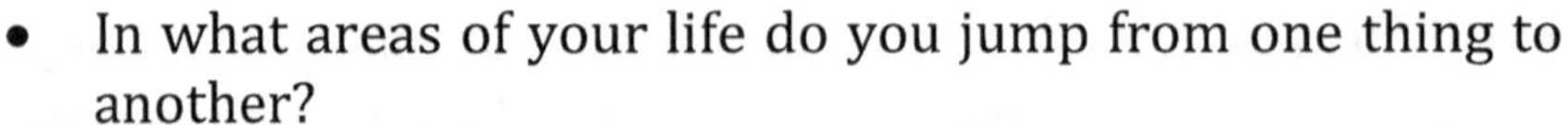

- In what areas of your life do you jump from one thing to another?

- Why do you think you're steadfast in some areas and not in others? How can you become more steadfast where needed?

PRAYER: Heavenly Father, forgive me when I rush into things or flit from project to project, even if—and especially if—those projects are done with you in mind. I so want to be steadfast; to focus on you. Please keep my eyes on you only. Please keep me steady and steadfast in my life so that I can fully live this life for your glory, shining like a star in the sky. Amen.

Day 15—I Know How to Wait

ത

Maybe all good things come to those that wait, but it's sure hard to wait.

Sometimes a crisis will explode in my life and I'm immediately up and at it. Trying to solve it. Trying to fix it. Trying to *do* something. Because it's so hard to wait. Yet, experience sometimes shows that the most important thing we should be doing when a crisis occurs is waiting. Stopping to pray. Stopping to breathe. Stopping to look at the situation from every angle. Stopping to ask for guidance, advice, help. Stopping to spend adequate time making a good decision based on everything we've learned to that point. Stopping to regain strength for the challenge ahead. Stopping to praise God for being in charge in it all and through it all, and sometimes, in spite of it all.

Esther was faced with the imminent annihilation of her people. That's a pretty big crisis to face. When Esther found out about Haman's evil plan though, she didn't jump up and run off to see the King. She moved slowly. First she consulted her uncle. Then she prayed and fasted for three days and asked the Jews in Susa to do the same. Only then did she approach the King.

But even when she approached the King she did not rush. She requested his presence at a banquet first. At the banquet, she patiently saw to the King's needs and comfort. Then again she refused to rush to express her need, even when he asked and said he would grant her request. She instead requested that the King and Haman return for a second banquet. Only at that second banquet did Esther make her plea to the King.

Don't you think King Xerxes was more than a little curious about what she wanted? Sure he was a king and enjoyed banquets, like any king would. But as king, he was also used to having people ask him for things. Constantly. Usually with accompanied demands based on greed or power. And usually they wanted things done right now, thank you very much.

To have to wait for Esther's request must have excited King Xerxes and made him more anxious to grant it, whatever it was. It also made the asking of it seem more important. Queen Esther's need was worth more than a quick request. It was worth the waiting; worth the preparation; worth the trouble Esther was going through. King Xerxes knew by the end of the first banquet that whatever Esther wanted was vital to her.

Important things are worth waiting for. Esther knew that this matter was too important to mess up by rushing through it. She knew that by waiting, she would have the King's full attention. She knew that by moving slowly, King Xerxes would also understand its importance.

How often in life do we rush through important things? Important decisions? Important processes? Often we feel we don't have enough time—even for the important things. How many things do you look back on and wish you had taken more time in the doing? The deciding? The experiencing?

Scripture reminds us of the need to take our time. To pray for guidance. To seek guidance from others. And especially to just wait on the Lord.

> *We wait in hope for the Lord; he is our help and our shield. In him our hearts rejoice, for we trust in his holy name. May your unfailing love be with us, Lord, even as we put our hope in you* (Psalm 33:20-22).
>
> *Be still and know that I am God* (Psalm 46:10).
>
> (See also Isaiah 40:31, Psalm 27:13-14, Psalm 37:34, James 5:7-8, 2 Peter 3:9, Psalm 130: 5-6)

I asked some friends about their thoughts about waiting. My friend Cora said that Paul is teaching her through Philippians to work on being content while waiting. My friend Dee said she is learning the difference between waiting and having patience. Being content, having patience, learning to be still are all part of the lesson Esther teaches us. Don't rush ahead of yourself. Especially, don't rush ahead of God.

Esther approached the King three times before she made her request. That gave her time to prepare her strength and resolve. It allowed time for God to prepare the King's heart and it allowed Haman time to prepare the things that became instrumental in his demise.

If Esther were here she would say this was her story. She understood the importance of taking time; of waiting for the time and the events to be right.

Who are we to God? When we practice patience and being still and waiting on God and His timing, we understand how He might see His women of faith. We can answer:

I am like Esther.

For Thought and Discussion

- Can you think of a time when something important happened in your life and you moved too quickly? What was the result?

- Was there an occasion when you took the time to address something important? How did you feel about the process? The outcome?

- How do you practice being still before God?

PRAYER: Heavenly Father, when things happen in my life that require action, please help me be patient and work through the process necessary to make the proper response. Please remind me to bring my important events to you first. Amen.

I am a Leader

Day 16—I Live in Community

ₔ

When my mother moved from a Christian-based assisted living community into a secular home, a common complaint was the "difference between the new location and the one where everyone was a Christian." Living in a community of believers makes a difference.

My brother became a monk late in life and moved in to a monastery. The monastery is not isolated from the world, but he lived in a community of believers. It was a place where everyone present had dedicated their lives to serving and worshipping God.

At home my husband and I read our Bible each day, pray, and read devotionals. We participate in a small group Bible study and attend church—because there is power, strength, and encouragement when you are part of a body of believers.

> *Go, gather together all the Jews who are in Susa, and fast for me. Do not eat or drink for three days, night or day. I and my attendants will fast as you do. When this is done, I will go to the king, even though it is against the law. And if I perish, I perish* (Esther 4:16).

Esther lived in a palace. She was surrounded by attendants and servants. And she—as queen—had them fast along with her. Perhaps her example and testimony led them to adopt her faith. Perhaps they were Jewish servants already. Whatever their background, Scripture tells us that they fasted with her—in community.

Additionally, Esther was part of a community of believers outside the palace walls. At her request, they joined her in fasting. They loved and supported her that way. And because Esther knew they were doing so, she was strengthened to do what she knew she would have to do. The love and support of a community of faith gave her courage and strength.

Scripture tells us that living in community with other believers strengthens us. *As iron sharpens iron, so one person sharpens another* (Proverbs 17:17). It also tells us that where there are *two or three gathered in my name, there am I* [Jesus] *with them* (Matthew 18:20, explanation added). And there is strength when believers are together: *A cord of three strands is not quickly broken* (Ecclesiastes 4:12).

> *And let us consider how to stir up one another to love and good works, not neglecting to meet together, as is the habit of some, but encouraging one another, and all the more as you see the Day drawing near* (Hebrews 10:24-25).

Being in a community is important, so we can stir up one another and do good works together. Also so that we can lift each other up and help each other when we are down.

> *Bear one another's burdens, and so fulfill the law of Christ* (Galatians 6:2).

Therefore encourage one another and build one another up, just as you are doing (1 Thessalonians 5:11).

Being part of a community of faith usually means being part of a local church. A church body of believers gather together to worship, learn, and grow in their faith. God continues to open our hearts to new revelations, continuing to grow us into the women He desires us to be. Has there ever been a time when the Pastor's message was exactly what you needed to hear? Even if you didn't want to hear it? Being part of a community of faith offers those opportunities to hear truths and be accountable for them.

There is something supernatural that happens when believers come together. We are a body of Christ. Because two or more are gathered in His name, He is there also. That means we can rely on someone else's faith when ours is weak. Have you known a person whose pain was so deep they could no longer find the strength or will to pray? When that happens, she can rely on the strength of another believer's faith. We can pray for each other. We can guide and support each other. We can strengthen each other. We can encourage each other so that the result is courage.

That is, that we may be mutually encouraged by each other's faith, both yours and mine (Romans 1:12).

Sometimes we have to make a decision that requires courage—where a principle is at stake; where we may have to stand alone. The reality is though, that even believers who live alone actually live in community, because a believer is never alone. The Holy Spirit is always with us. We can therefore always be in communion with God. Those two or more gathered together? They might be just you and the Holy Spirit.

If Esther were here she would say this was her story. Even though she lived in the palace, she remained a part of a community of believers. She knew that being part of a community of believers strengthened her faith.

Who are we to God? When we realize the power and joy of living in community with other believers, we understand how God might see His women of faith. We can answer:

I am like Esther.

For Thought and Discussion

- Do you know someone who is not a believer? Who does she turn to for advice? Who helps her in times of trial or crisis?

- Are you presently part of a church community? What has been your experience fellowshipping with other believers?

- Do you sense the presence of the Holy Spirit in your life? Are you open to His leading? How might you better attune your heart to listen for the Spirit's presence?

PRAYER: Heavenly Father, thank you for being always with me always. I know from the Bible that the Holy Spirit lives within me. Sometimes though I can't sense your presence. Please show me how to be still and recognize that you are with me in a real way. Help me live in community with you daily and also with other believers. Amen.

Day 17—I Focus on Others

When my mother-in-law was dying, my sister-in-law asked family members to help with her hospice care. My sister-in-law is a registered nurse. Me? I'm a mom. And that's the extent of my medical training.

I was tempted to decline to help. Really, what did I know about caring for a dying person? And how could I hope to bring cheer and comfort when I was in such despair over losing my wonderful mother-in-law? On the other hand, it was my very last chance to "do" for my mother-in-law on this side of Heaven. How could I decline?

Ultimately, caring for my sweet Rosemary was a gift to me. When I focused not on my grief but on the gift that her life was to me and the joy in knowing that I would truly, really, for absolute certain see her again with Jesus, the despair turned to gratitude for the opportunity to care for her physical needs and to give thanksgiving for her life. The time I spent with Rosemary became a time to focus on family, on helping my sister-in-law care for the woman we both loved; a time to focus not on myself but on the needs of others.

And I was blessed beyond all expectation.

> *I will go to the king, even though it is against the law. And if I perish, I perish* (Esther 4:16).

Esther was a young woman. She had been shielded as a child. Now she was protected within the sturdy palace walls. She was afraid for what she knew must be done. Perhaps she could have saved herself from the pending slaughter by keeping silent and not causing controversy. But she knew that her focus needed to be outside of herself and beyond her personal needs. She knew there was something bigger at stake. Her focus became the plight of others.

As Christians, we are admonished to focus our attention on others, too. Do unto others as you would have them do unto you. Love one another. In fact, we are to care more about others than we do ourselves; treat others better than we are treated.

> *Speak up for those who cannot speak for themselves, for the rights of all who are destitute* (Proverbs 31:8).

> *Learn to do right; seek justice. Defend the oppressed* (Isaiah 1:17).

I especially love Philippians 2:3: *Do nothing out of selfish ambition or vain conceit. Rather, in humility value others above yourselves.*

Our focus should be outward. Paul urges us to practice hospitality (Romans 12:13). Peter tells us to show hospitality to one another *without grumbling* (1 Peter 4:9). We are to build each other up (1 Thessalonians 5:11); be kind to one another (Ephesians 4:32), look to the interests of others (Philippians 2:4), welcome one another (Romans 15:2-7) and seek not our own good but the good of our neighbor (1 Corinthians 10:24). In other words, again and again Scripture reminds us to love God and love one another as Jesus commanded (Matthew 22:37-39; Mark 12:30-31; Luke 10:27).

Like Esther, we need to understand that there is something bigger at stake than our personal comfort, priorities or desires. What is at stake is God's plan. Our focus should be on His plan and on other people; rather than on ourselves. Esther learned that lesson and as a result, God's plan prevailed.

If Esther were here she would say this was her story. She set aside her own fears and focused on the needs of others.

Who are we to God? When we recognize the importance and blessings in setting aside our own desires and focusing outside of ourselves we understand how God might see His women of faith. We can answer:

I am like Esther.

For Thought and Discussion

- Think of a time your life was in crisis. Did you focus entirely upon yourself? How did you feel during that time?

- Think of a time when your life was in crisis but you focused on other people. How did that affect your own sense of worry and despair?

- How could you try to remember to focus on others when you are going through troubles in the future?

PRAYER: Heavenly Father, we recognize that you desire us to grow in faith from our trials. Please help us not to focus solely on ourselves when trials occur. Teach us how to bless others by what we are going through; to reach out and love others in your name so that you can use even our trials to love others through us. Amen.

Day 18—I am Courageous

ര്യ

I think about the personality characteristics that make me who I am. Fear is always one of the biggies. I lack confidence; I'm afraid to try something new; I worry that people will judge me and find me lacking. I'm afraid.

But when I look at my life from the outside, I see that I have snorkeled in five countries of the world even though I cannot swim. I have become an author of traditionally published books even though I had no formal writing training. I formed a professional speakers group even though I—like everyone else in the world—am terrified of public speaking. How can I call myself afraid when I purposely do the things I am most afraid to do? It's because I have courage.

Courage is not the absence of fear. Courage recognizes fear and allows you to do what you're afraid of anyway. Our first reaction to most new situations is often fear. But our second reactions are prompted by the advice of others, by circumstances, by pressures from outside, by waiting on God.

Esther's first reaction to the news of her people's impending slaughter and what Mordecai asked her to do was fear. She responded:

> *All the king's officials and the people of the royal provinces know that for any man or woman who approaches the king in the inner court without being summoned the king has but one law: that they be put to death unless the king extends the gold scepter to them and spares their lives. But thirty days have passed since I was called to go to the king* (Esther 4:11).

In other words, Esther said, "Wait a minute! Everybody knows I can't talk to the King unless he asks for me. He'll kill me if I do that. And he hasn't even wanted to see me for a month. Maybe he doesn't even like me anymore."

But Mordecai reminded Esther of her duty to her people and the unique position she held in the kingdom. With Mordecai's reminder, Esther saw her duty clearly. Because her duty overrode her fear, she was able to summon courage, saying: *"So I will go in unto the king, which is not according to the law: and if I perish, I perish"* (Esther 4:16).

Esther was the original Wonder Woman. She had courage, even though she was afraid. Esther had justifiable reasons to be afraid beyond the stated law. Her position as queen was the direct result of Queen Vashti's disobedience to the very king Esther was now planning to approach in a manner that was against the law.

Esther is an example of heroism of the unheroic. She had a valid fear. She faced the very real possibility of death if she approached the King. She looked for another way out. But when she realized there was none, she did what was needed. It does not take courage to do something that is convenient, comfortable or easy. But it does take courage to do something difficult or scary.

It takes tremendous courage to do something that might cost you your physical life.

Scripture is filled with examples of heroism—from Moses leading God's people through the Red Sea, to David facing a giant with a handful of rocks, to the prophets standing firm amid persecution and confrontation and relating what God wanted them to tell. In each instance, the person needed courage to do what God asked him to do. And in each instance, God gave the person enough courage to complete the assigned task.

Paul later put this into words to live by: *I can do all things through Christ who strengthens me* (Philippians 4:13).

God doesn't just give us physical strength. He doesn't just give us emotional strength or spiritual strength. God also gives us courage. Courage to stand before the king and tell him what he needs to know to be able to do the right thing. God gave Esther that kind of courage. He gives us that kind of courage, too. If only we ask.

When Joshua was preparing to lead the Israelites into the Promised Land, facing the people who already lived there, God told him to be strong and courageous. God's words to Joshua still ring true.

> *Do not fear or be in dread of them, for it is the Lord your God who goes with you. He will not leave you or forsake you* (Joshua 1:9).

This is repeated in Psalms.

> *I have set the Lord always before me; because he is at my right hand, I shall not be shaken* (Psalm 16:8).

In ancient Jewish symbolism, the right hand is the hand that represents power. Jesus sits at the right hand of the Father. Jesus sits at the hand of power. Jesus also sits at our right hand.

We have access to the very power of Jesus. Having the power of Jesus available to us should give us the courage we need for every task He asks us to accomplish.

Sometimes, that courage we need? It's the courage to ask God to help us do the right thing. That right thing is His will, even if we think we know better or want something different. Sometimes it's about having the courage to set aside our own ideas and allow God to work. That courage comes from trusting Him. Trusting Him comes from the very fact that He alone is trustworthy.

If Esther were here she would say this was her story. She was afraid but did what she needed to do anyway.

Who are we to God? When we realize that God can give us the courage to accomplish what we fear to do, we know how He might see His women of faith. We can answer:

I am like Esther.

For Thought and Discussion

- Think of when you were afraid to do something and did it anyway. Was it easier the next time you needed courage?

- What is the most courageous thing you've ever seen? Why did it seem so courageous to you?

- How might Philippians 4:13 give you courage next time you need it?

PRAYER: Heavenly Father, I sometimes let fear take over my life. I know you don't desire me to live in fear. So many times in the Bible you and your angels tell people "Do not be afraid." Please remind me that even the patriarchs needed courage and that you stand ready to fill me with that courage if only I ask. Amen.

Day 19—I Stand in the Inner Court

ꕥ

There's an imaginary doggie gate at the bottom of our stairs. Our downstairs flooring is tile-covered doggie central. The pooches know that downstairs is their domain. But the carpeted upstairs is special. To go upstairs requires an invitation. Upstairs is the "inner court" in the Peterson Palace. Our puppy dogs know they are only allowed access upstairs by the gracious granting of their human kings.

> *On the third day Esther put on her royal robes and stood in the inner court of the palace, in front of the king's hall. The king was sitting on his royal throne in the hall, facing the entrance. When he saw Queen Esther standing in the court, he was pleased with her and held out to her the gold scepter that was in his hand. So Esther approached and touched the tip of the scepter* (Esther 5:1).

In King Xerxes palace, no one was allowed into the presence of the King without permission. That rule extended to both the throne room and the inner court. It meant that a person had to have been summoned first to the inner court. Stage one. Only then *might* the person be granted further permission to personally approach the throne. Both steps were dependent upon the whim of the King. Should the King decide the answer was "no," it resulted in immediate death to the person wanting an audience with him. That rule was law in the Persian Empire.

The Jews before Jesus' time were not allowed into the innermost chamber of the Temple. The Holy Place could only be entered by a priest. Everyone else, no matter how godly and righteous, was excluded from God's presence. The priests alone were allowed to mediate with God on behalf of the Jewish people. They alone were allowed to enter the inner court.

Moreover, it was within that Holy of Holies place, behind the second curtain where the Ark of the Covenant was kept. It was in the Ark of the Covenant that the Jewish people believed God was present.

> *There, above the cover between the two cherubim that are over the ark of the covenant law, I will meet with you and give you all my commands for the Israelites* (Exodus 25:22).

Back then, God separated His presence from ours by keeping mankind out from the Holy of Holies; the Most Holy Place. Only one man from one tribe of Jews was allowed into God's presence one time each year to mediate on behalf of His people (Hebrews 9:7).

Then came Jesus. We no longer were kept away from the presence of God. Paul says:

> *Therefore, brothers and sisters, since we have confidence to enter the Most Holy Place by the blood of Jesus, by a new and living way opened for us through the curtain, that is, his body, and since we*

> *have a great priest over the house of God, let us draw near to God with a sincere heart and with the full assurance that faith brings, having our hearts sprinkled to cleanse us from a guilty conscience and having our bodies washed with pure water. Let us hold unswervingly to the hope we profess, for he who promised is faithful* (Hebrews 10:19-23).

When Jesus died, the physical curtain and the theological curtain between the outer temple and the inner court in the Jewish Temple were torn apart (See Matthew 27:51 and Mark 15:38). The curtain separating the rest of the Temple with the place God resided was no longer needed. Jesus himself became our mediator. For the first time, everyone who called upon God could do so in the name of Jesus—personally—stepping into the inner court and standing in His presence.

> *For Christ has entered, not into holy places made with hands, which are copies of the true things, but into heaven itself, now to appear in the presence of God on our behalf* (Hebrews 9:24).

As a member of King Jesus' family, we can stand in God's presence in the inner court. The only invitation we need is the one He has given to all people for all time. "Come to me." We can stand in the inner court in confidence because Jesus stands there with us. And He is pleased to see us there.

If Esther were here she would say this was her story. Her king gladly allowed her to stand in the inner court.

Who are we to God? When we realize that God allows us to stand in His inner court and is happy to see us there, we understand how He might see His women of faith. We can answer:

I am like Esther.

For Thought and Discussion

- Picture the scene in ancient Israel where only one member from the tribe of Levi—the High Priest—could approach God and only one time each year. How would you feel knowing we would have been isolated from God?

- How do you feel knowing you have immediate and intimate access to the King of Heaven because of Jesus?

- Does this knowledge of your access to Jesus humble you or make Him feel like a friend?

PRAYER: Heavenly Father, thank you for your plan. I worship you with thanksgiving for the holy God you are. But I also praise you and thank you for making a way for me to come into your presence and be close to you. Thank you for loving me that much. Amen.

Day 20—I Can Approach the Throne

When you pray, do you pray to God the Father? To Jesus? Or to the Holy Spirit? Or do you—like me—sometimes pray individually to the different persons of the Trinity in turn? Some people say they pray to Abba Father. Others only pray to Jesus. Many people chuckle at my question and respond that, sometimes they feel insecure about praying in general and fall back on the generic "Dear Lord."

The good thing about praying to our Almighty God is that He is the Trinity: God the Father, God the Son, and God the Holy Spirit. And He is Lord of all. When you pray to one, you pray to all. So, while I like to address my prayers to which person of the Trinity *I think* is in charge of that particular issue, underneath it all *I know* that the *to whom* is less relevant than that I have approached the Throne of God and that I have His ear. In other words, when I pray, God hears me.

> *On the third day Esther put on her royal robes and stood in the inner court of the palace, in front of the king's hall. The king was sitting on his royal throne in the hall, facing the entrance. When he saw Queen*

> *Esther standing in the court, he was pleased with her and held out to her the gold scepter that was in his hand. So Esther approached and touched the tip of the scepter* (Esther 5:1).

Esther went to see the King. She stood in the inner court and waited for him to see her. Then she approached the throne in confidence; knowing that by holding out his scepter, King Xerxes had granted Esther an audience. More than that, he granted her life. She then knew that she was loved by the King. The significance of King Xerxes' invitation to Esther to join him at the throne is that her visit became personal. She no longer had to stand away from him but was invited personally into his presence.

Scripture is filled with imagery and visions the prophets shared about the throne of God. Here are a few.

> *Then I saw a great white throne and him who was seated on it* (Revelation 20:11).

> *Thus says the Lord: "Heaven is my throne, and the earth is my footstool; what is the house that you would build for me, and what is the place of my rest?"* (Isaiah 14:13).

> *In the year that King Uzziah died I saw the Lord sitting upon a throne, high and lifted up; and the train of his robe filled the temple* (Isaiah 6:1).

> *Your throne, O God, will last for ever and ever; a scepter of justice will be the scepter of your kingdom* (Psalm 45:6).

In the time before Jesus' earthly life, only one part of one tribe of Jews was allowed to come into the presence of our Holy God. Then Jesus came and held out His scepter to us for all time.

By doing so, King Jesus granted us an audience. He granted us eternal life. He showed us that He loved us and allowed us to approach the throne so that we could stand in His presence.

> *Let us then approach God's throne of grace with confidence, so that we may receive mercy and find grace to help us in our time of need* (Hebrews 4:16).

First Jesus became our mediator, doing away with a need for us to be separated from God. Then He invited us personally to come into His presence so that we might have a one-on-one relationship—King and beloved Bride and friend.

If Esther were here she would say this was her story. Because of the King's love for her she was able to approach his throne.

Who are we to God? When we realize God loves us so much that He has held out His scepter to us to enable us to approach His throne in confidence, we can answer:

I am like Esther.

For Thought and Discussion

- How would your prayer life be different if Jesus had not made it possible to pray directly to and through him?

- Picture sitting at Jesus' feet in adoration. What does His throne look like in your imagination? What does His scepter look like?

- Have you tried praying to the different persons of the Trinity? Would doing so help you understand the character and power of God?

PRAYER: Holy God, you are so mighty and worthy to be praised. Thank you for making a way that I might come into your presence. Thank you for making a way for me to approach your throne with confidence. Amen.

Day 21—I See My Duty

ᘓᘓ

Imagine an off-duty police officer who comes upon a man assaulting a woman on the street. Does he turn away, noting that he's done his 8-hour shift and it's not his problem? Does he phone 9-1-1 and leave it at that? Probably not. More likely the off-duty police officer would intervene. Even though he's legally "off duty," he's still a police officer.

Imagine a doctor, off duty from the hospital. He comes upon a vehicle accident with injured people on the scene. Does he drive on or turn away? Or does he stop and help? Most likely he would feel it was his duty to help.

Imagine a mother seeing a child crying alone in the store, obviously separated from his mother. Does she turn away, thinking the mother should keep better watch on her children? More likely, she stops and leads the child to a clerk who can call for the child's mother on the store intercom. Or she stays with the child and comforts him until his mother returns. It is her mother's duty to help.

Esther was a young Jewess. That didn't change when she became Queen. It simply meant she was a Jewess who now held a special position in society. As a Jewess, she still had a duty to her people. In fact, as a Jewess in a position of power, she now held an even higher duty to her people.

If Esther had not been Queen, but had still been living with Mordecai when the day came that enemies of the Jews attacked, would not she have helped Mordecai and her neighbors prepare? Would not she have helped block the doors? Would not she have aided the injured? Would not she have prayed over and comforted the dying? It would have been her duty as a member of her community.

> *And who knows but that you have come to royal position for such a time as this?* (Esther: 4:14)

Just so, as queen, Esther maintained a duty to help her people. But now, she held a position that enabled her to do her duty in a unique way. Other young Jewesses could prepare, block the doors, aid the injured, and comfort the dying. Esther had new duties to carry out as a Queen of the Persian Empire who was also a Jew. Esther remembered her duty and performed it regardless of and because of her new circumstances.

God has given each of us special circumstances and gifts. He expects us to use our gifts within those circumstances. It is our duty to do so.

> *Each of you should use whatever gift you have received to serve others, as faithful stewards of God's grace in its various forms* (1 Peter 4:10).

In addition, we should be aware of the manner in which we serve, remembering that, just as Jesus came to serve, so should we do our duty as a servant of God, according to Jesus' parable of the man whose servant prepared dinner.

> *"Will he thank the servant because he did what he was told to do? So you also, when you have done everything you were told to do, should say, 'We are unworthy servants; we have only done our duty'"* (Luke 17:8-10).

Sometimes, our modern minds can't get around the idea that being a servant is a good thing. But Jesus Himself said that he came not to be served but to serve others (Matthew 20:28 and Mark 10:45). Being a servant of God is a really good thing. Moreover, serving results in a blessing. The last time Jesus was with His disciples before He was crucified, He washed their feet, giving them an example of service to others. Then He said:

> *Very truly I tell you, no servant is greater than his master, nor is a messenger greater than the one who sent him. Now that you know these things,* ***you will be blessed if you do them*** (John 13:16-17, emphasis added).

We will be blessed by serving others. Now as well as in eternity. The greatest joy will be for those who stand before Jesus in Heaven and to whom He says: "Well done, good and faithful servant" (Matthew 25:21).

We have a duty to use our gifts in a way that honors God. We have a duty to serve others. We have a duty to share Jesus with others. Jesus gave us this duty when He commissioned us.

> *Therefore go and make disciples of all nations, baptizing them in the name of the Father and of the Son and of the Holy Spirit, and teaching them to obey everything I have commanded you. And surely I am with you always, to the very end of the age"* (Matthew 28:19-20).

If Esther were here she would say this was her story. She knew her duty and fulfilled it, regardless of the consequences.

Who are we to God? When we recognize that God expects us to see our duty, to use our gifts, to serve others, and to share the Gospel, we understand how He might see His women of faith. We can answer:

I am like Esther.

For Thought and Discussion

- What are some of your duties? Are they duties required by law? Family? Duties as a friend? Citizen? How do you maintain these duties?

- Do you generally live up to the duties entrusted to you or seek ways to avoid them?

- What duties do you have as a Christian? Are there any Christian duties you are trying to avoid?

PRAYER: Heavenly Father, I acknowledge that you have given me responsibilities in my life and that my duty as a Christian to follow you never changes, even if my circumstances do. Please help me see and do my duty each day. As I become better at doing my duty, please give me more responsibility as you deem appropriate. Help me grow in you. Amen.

Day 22—I Accept My Role

One of my favorite Julie Andrews' movies was *Thoroughly Modern Millie*. I loved the way Millie Dillmount took hold of her role as a modern woman at the start of the twentieth century. I loved that she set out to have a career and to embody a strong, independent, and vivacious woman.

Let's face it: women in ancient times had little real power or rights. They were expected to be submissive to their husbands, their king, and the restrictive rules of society. Even though Esther was made queen, her husband, King Xerxes held the real power. She knew that fact and gave herself fully to her role—whatever it was to become.

In Chapter 9 of the book of Esther we see something amazing; something unusual for the political climate of the time.

> *So Queen Esther, daughter of Abihail, along with Mordecai the Jew, wrote with full authority to confirm this second letter concerning Purim. And Mordecai sent letters to all the Jews in the 127 provinces of Xerxes' kingdom—words of goodwill*

> *and assurance— to establish these days of Purim at their designated times, as Mordecai the Jew and Queen Esther had decreed for them, and as they had established for themselves and their descendants in regard to their times of fasting and lamentation.* ***Esther's decree*** *confirmed these regulations about Purim, and it was written down in the records* (Esther 9:29-32, emphasis added).

Did you see it? Look at the words: *Esther's decree*. Esther, orphaned Jewess made Queen of the Persian Empire, but more shockingly—a mere woman—made an official, legally binding decree that was written down in the official records of the empire. Those records are also part of the history of the Jewish people and her action was preserved in Scripture for all time.

An ancient woman who makes a decree? An ancient woman whose decree is recorded? There is no evidence that Queen Esther ever aspired to political greatness. She expected no personal glory to come from what she did. But she gave herself over to her role as Queen, all the while being submissive to those in authority over her. And she was honored throughout history as a person important to her people and to the empire led by her husband the King.

Esther had no foreknowledge of what would be required of her. She simply met each demand as it came. She was taken into the harem and did her best to prepare to be pleasing to the King. When she was made Queen, Esther accepted her new role. When Mordecai asked her to speak with the King, she prayerfully complied. Esther took what came and did what was needed. She was strong *amid* her submissiveness.

Modern women sometimes feel that Scripture portrays women as weak and without power. But the Bible has preserved the lives of dozens of women, such as Esther, who were strong and self-determining. Moreover, Proverbs 31 describes the perfect wife—the wife of noble character. Not only does a Proverbs wife take care of her family, she buys property, plants crops, and runs a profitable business. She is to be honored.

Rebekah drew enough water to fill Abraham's servant's camels (Genesis 24:19-20). If one camel can drink more than 50 gallons of water in three minutes, Rebekah had to have been a strong woman! Rahab was a spy (Joshua 2). Deborah was a judge who led an army (Judges 4). Lydia was a business woman (Acts 16). We could argue that any one of those women would be seen as strong and independent even by today's standards.

Moreover, each of us have a role to play in the Church. Paul talks about the body of the Church and that each person contributes in a unique way. He likens our physical bodies to the Church's various parts, noting that our arms are not more important than our feet but that all parts are needed. Similarly, we all contribute to the strength of the Church.

> *Now you are the body of Christ, and each one of you is a part of it* (1 Corinthians 12:27).

If Esther were here she would say this was her story. She accepted her roles as they were placed upon her and maintained her strength even at times when she was obedient to others.

Who are we to God? When we realize how to be strong within the confines of our roles and that we each have a role to play within the body of Christ, we understand how God might see His women of faith. We can answer:

I am like Esther.

For Thought and Discussion

- Do you know any women who have great inner strength yet know how to allow others to lead? Are you one of those women?

- Do you believe you can be both strong and submissive? Why or why not?

- In what areas of your life do you need to be more of a leader? In what areas do you need to be more submissive?

PRAYER: Heavenly Father, you know my heart and understand that I want to be strong. You also understand that our society has steeled us against the idea of submission to anyone—even you. Please lead my understanding to know and accept what you mean and to always be submissive to you, dear Lord. Amen.

I Know God is Good

Day 23—I Trust in God's Justice

A favorite family saying comes from my mother-in-law. One day when Jim complained that "it" wasn't fair, she replied: "Who ever said life was fair?" Although I recognize the truth in it, sometimes I really hate that it is true. I like fairness. After all, it's equitable, just, and so very . . . fair.

Do you ever feel life isn't fair? Like some days you are cheated? Maybe you don't receive the accolades, praise, or benefits you deserve. It is common in today's society to not only want things to be fair. We also have come to believe we are entitled to free money, opportunities, and "stuff." But that sentiment is not justice. True justice comes only from God. He is the ultimate judge. Only He knows what is best and right. And that justice may not always fit in with what our society sees as "fair."

Some Christians don't think it's fair that a life-long sinner should get the reward of heaven if he repents on his deathbed. We forget that seeking forgiveness, repenting, and being granted salvation—for whatever time a person is a Christian on this earth—is justice in God's eyes. And we also forget that neither do we deserve the grace and mercy that God has given us—

unworthy though we are. In other words, we often can't understand what justice means to God because we're so busy rationalizing it from our human perspective.

Esther sought justice. From a human point of view, she wanted things to be fair.

> *The Jews assembled in their cities in all the provinces of King Xerxes to attack those determined to destroy them* (Esther 9:2).

In other words, the Jews didn't set out to kill everyone. They only sought to protect themselves from those who were "determined to destroy them." Not revenge, not brutality for the sake of brutality. Defense. Justice. Fairness. That was the decree created by Esther and her cousin Mordecai.

Yes, King Xerxes also put Haman's ten sons to death. But that too—from the view of an ancient world where sons had a familial obligation to carry out retribution on behalf of their family—was seen as fair and just in order to prevent future violence against the King and the Jewish people.

Within the Citadel of Susa and in the outlying regions of the Empire, the Jews struck down and killed their enemies who sought to destroy them. But the accounts of Chapter 9, verses 10, 15, and 16 further tell us that *they did not lay their hands on the plunder.* The custom of the times said that victors were allowed (and expected) to take the possessions of the enemies they vanquished. But in this case, even though the enemies of the Jews had sought to destroy them, the Jews did not take what was rightfully theirs by custom.

In fact, from a biblical historical point of view, the not taking plunder also theologically reverses the error made by King Saul. At that time, King Saul had taken plunder from the

Amalekites instead of destroying it. That action had contradicted God's explicit command to take no plunder (1 Samuel 15:3, 9).[8]

Esther also sought justice from God's point of view. Although Esther put things in motion that resulted in the deliverance of her people, over and through it all she trusted in God's justice. Through prayer and fasting, Esther knew that God would be the one to provide deliverance. She didn't seek God's retribution. She sought His justice. How do we know this? When Esther went to the King, she did not seek vengeance. Rather her first request was to ask the King to repeal his decree.

But the laws of the Persian Empire did not allow the King to repeal a decree. There was no longer a legal possibility to return to the way things were. So instead, Esther sought fairness. It wasn't fair that her people stand there and be slaughtered. More fair would be that her people be allowed to arm and defend themselves. Esther saw injustice. When human laws prevented the King from repealing his edict, Esther and Mordecai created a new decree to return justice to an unjust situation.

It doesn't feel fair when we look at the world and see the wicked prosper. We have to remember that ultimately God's justice prevails; whether in our lifetime or not.

> *For God will bring every deed into judgment, including every hidden thing, whether it is good or evil* (Ecclesiastes 12:14).

> *Beloved, never avenge yourselves, but leave it to the wrath of God, for it is written, "Vengeance is mine, I will repay, says the Lord"* (Romans 12:19).

> *Judge not, that you will be not judged. For with the judgment you pronounce you will be judged, and*

[8] Ortlund, *ESV Exhaustive Commentary,* 284.

> *with the measure you use it will be measured to you* (Matthew 7:1-2).
>
> *Forgive us our sins, as (in the amount, to the extent, just as) we forgive those who sin against us* (Luke 11:4, explanation added).

We don't have to worry about justice because God will take care of everything. God's providence doesn't require high visibility. God doesn't shout "did you see me at work today?" He whispers; sometimes He works in silence.

If Esther were here she would say this was her story. She sought justice rather than vengeance, trusting God through it all.

Who are we to God? When we seek justice but recognize that ultimate justice comes only from God, we understand how God might see His women of faith. We can answer:

I am like Esther.

For Thought and Discussion

- How does your sense of "fairness" affect your thinking about politics, faith, salvation, life in general?

- Are you able to see when you have wronged someone else—even unintentionally? How have those realizations grown your faith?

- How does God's justice make you feel as it relates to your salvation and the salvation of others?

PRAYER: Heavenly Father, thank you that you are ultimately and completely just. Thank you even more that you grant me grace rather than the justice I deserve and that you grant me mercy rather than the punishment I deserve. Amen.

Day 24—I Humble Myself

I'm a writer. I'm also a mom and a sister, a daughter, a house cleaner, a laundress, a cook, and an accountant. But when people find out I've got published books, for some reason they think that makes me smarter somehow. Uh . . . no, it just means I can type fast and have a lot to say. In fact, when my first book was published, I held no giant book launch party. Didn't do a book signing. I opened the box, took out one of my babies, flipped through it and said, "I can't believe I typed all these words myself."

Not what you'd expect to hear if I thought I was *all that.*

It's the way it is with many published writers. We mostly feel incredibly honored that someone would pay us for the words we've put together. A publishing house would spend money to bind them into a book. People would buy them, take them into their homes where their loved ones reside, open them, and read all of those words. Wow. Thank you, readers for doing that. When you think of how people spend their precious time and brain cells with something that has come from my feeble brain—it is a very humbling experience.

Esther too was humble. Even though she had been recognized as one of the Empire's most beautiful women, even though the King had selected her from the hundreds of other young women brought before him; even though he had placed the royal crown upon her lovely head—still she was humble before him and before others.

When Esther went to visit the King, he held his scepter out to her and spared her life. Moreover, the King was anxious to grant whatever request she had come to ask. She knew he valued her life. And now she had the attention and consideration of the King of the Persian Empire.

But still Esther moved slowly. At the beginning of the crisis, it never occurred to her that she knew what to do on her own. Before going to the King, she requested prayer from the Jewish community. She sought advice from her cousin. When she was received into the inner court, she continued to move slowly, inviting the King—and Haman—to a banquet.

Once she had them in her quarters, she again moved slowly. She asked for nothing more than the opportunity to entertain and feed them once more. At that second dinner, did she then wield her power? No. She fell at the King's feet. She humbly told him she was to be slain.

> *If I have found favor with you, O king, and if it pleases your majesty, grant me my life—this is my petition. And spare my people—this is my request* (Esther 7:3).

Esther did not moan or wail. She did not beg or plead or try to use her wiles to twist the King's emotions. She humbled herself and left the judgment to the King.

We don't know what Esther's first thoughts were when she found out that the Jews were to be slaughtered. But it was her second thoughts prompted by Mordecai that caused Esther to act as she did. In our lives, often our first instincts are irrational or poorly thought through. It is when we obtain the wisdom and advice of others, when we rely on circumstances and experiences, when we weigh pressures from outside, and when we wait on God that we are able to take ourselves out of the picture and humbly adopt a plan that is better than our own would have ever been.

> *God opposes the proud but shows favor to the humble* (James 4:6).

One of the greatest patriarchs in Scripture was Moses. The first five books of the Old Testament are purportedly written by Moses. How did God see Moses?

> *Now Moses was a very humble man, more humble than anyone else on the face of the earth* (Numbers 12:3).

Moses was humble. Yet God used Moses in a big way. And God loved Moses—enough to allow Moses into His very presence, commissioning Moses with deliverance of the Jewish people from Egypt, and entrusting him to record God's law for all time.

Here are a few more verses about humility.

> *For though the LORD is high, he regards the lowly, but the haughty he knows from afar* (Psalm 138:6).

> *The reward for humility and fear of the LORD is riches and honor and life* (Proverbs 22:5).

> *Do nothing from rivalry or conceit, but in humility count others more significant than yourselves* (Philippians 2:3).

> *With all humility and gentleness, with patience, bearing with one another in love* (Ephesians 4:2).

> *Finally, all of you, have unity of mind, sympathy, brotherly love, a tender heart, and a humble mind* (1 Peter 3:8).

> *But he gives us more grace. That is why Scripture says: "God opposes the proud but shows favor to the humble"* (James 4:6).

> *For all those who exalt themselves will be humbled, and those who humble themselves will be exalted* (Luke 14:11).

> *Humble yourselves, therefore, under God's mighty hand, that he may lift you up in due time* (1 Peter 5:6).

God wants us to be humble before Him. He wants us to present our requests to Him; not arrogantly; but with humility and trust in His ultimate authority. Just as Esther approached King Xerxes, so should we present our requests in deference to God's wisdom, His plan, and His power. Just as Jesus prayed, "not my will, but yours" (Luke 22:42), so too, should we humbly present our requests to God and trust in His authority and wisdom.

If Esther were here she would say this was her story. She humbled herself before her King.

Who are we to God? When we know how to humble ourselves before God, we understand how God might see His women of faith. We can answer:

I am like Esther.

For Thought and Discussion

- In what ways do you need to humble yourself before God?

- In what ways do you need to humble yourself before others?

- Who do you have in your community of faith who can offer you wise counsel? Do you seek it? Do you follow it?

PRAYER: Heavenly Father, I love you so much that sometimes I take pride in my faith. Sometimes it makes me not righteous, but self-righteous. Please forgive me and show me how to return to humility and be humble before you and others. Amen.

Day 25—I am Abundantly Blessed

ঌ৹ও

When our children were little, we sought to teach them about financial planning. One of the things we wanted them to do was read the classic book on wealth, *The Richest Man in Babylon* by George S. Classon. Although each story in the book is short in length, the writing is old-style with descriptive words and lengthy narratives. It's a difficult book for beginning readers to dig their way through. But my husband felt the book was important for the kids to read. It was worth a little bribery. So he promised each of them $10 if they read the book; more if they gave a report to the family on what they'd learned from it.

Both children read the book and gave a little report on what it said. At the end of their reports, they asked for their reward. Jim handed them each $10 for the reading and then asked them what would be a fair reward for the extra report. They thought about it a while. Our son suggested another $5.00. Our daughter—for whom the ordeal was more trying at three years younger than big brother—suggested an additional $10 would be appropriate.

Jim handed each of them a crisp new $100 bill. To this day, our daughter is able to recite part of one of the stories from the book. Both kids are excellent money managers and savers. That $100 bill was an extravagant gift. And worth every penny in the lessons learned. The point though is that our desire was for our children to learn something that would be valuable to them. And we rewarded them abundantly; blessing them tremendously more than they expected. And if you were wondering, yes, the $100 went into their savings accounts.

It was King Xerxes' desire to abundantly bless Queen Esther.

> *Then the king asked, "What is it, Queen Esther? What is your request? Even up to half the kingdom, it will be given you"* (Esther 5:3).

The King said this to Esther three times; first in Esther 5:3, again at Esther's first banquet (Esther 5:6) and again at the second banquet (Esther 7:2). The King's response to beautiful Queen Esther was consistent: he offered her abundant generosity.

Peter writes:

> *And God is able to bless you abundantly, so that in all things at all times, having all that you need, you will abound in every good work* (2 Corinthians 9:8).

Similarly, Jesus says: *I have come that they may have life, and have it to the full* (John 10:10). And: *ask and it shall be given you* (Matthew 7:6). Need a few more verses about God's abundant generosity?

> *And my God will meet all your needs according to the riches of his glory in Christ Jesus* (Philippians 4:19).

> *Every good and perfect gift is from above, coming down from the Father of the heavenly lights, who does not change like shifting shadows* (James 1:17).

> *Give, and it will be given to you. A good measure, pressed down, shaken together and running over, will be poured into your lap. For with the measure you use, it will be measured to you* (Luke 6:38).

> *For the Lord God is a sun and shield; the Lord bestows favor and honor; no good thing does he withhold from those whose walk is blameless* (Psalm 84:11).

And don't forget the Beatitudes from Jesus' Sermon on the Mount (Matthew 5). Each of those things we learn—right from the very first blessing about being poor in spirit and recognizing that our salvation can't be earned but is given freely through Jesus—those are amazing, abundant, and eternal blessings we will only fully appreciate on the other side of eternity. And maybe not even fully then.

Just as we delight in giving joy to our children, so God delights in blessing us. And not just bless us, but bless us abundantly, with overwhelming generosity, just as King Xerxes desired to bless Queen Esther.

If Esther were here she would say this was her story. She knew that her King desired to bless her abundantly.

Who are we to God? When we realize how abundantly God wants to bless and when we acknowledge His blessings with deep gratitude, we understand how He might see His women of faith. We can answer:

I am like Esther.

For Thought and Discussion

- In what areas of your life do you not only feel blessed, but *abundantly blessed*?

- In what areas of your life do you try to abundantly bless others?

- In what areas of your life could you be doing more blessing of others?

PRAYER: Heavenly Father, thank you for your blessings. Forgive me when I take them for granted. Thank you also for the blessings I don't even understand—those miracles and plans and God-things you do that are beyond my comprehension. Please help me always remember your greatest blessing, Jesus—that of your love and salvation. Amen.

Day 26—I Celebrate God's Deliverance

Do you have a happy dance—one of those silly, hopping, swinging, twirling, stomping things you do when something goes particularly right?

For me, part of the fun of watching football are the happy dances those big, hulking guys do after a touchdown. Those guys are so manly with their bulking muscles and enormously padded man bodies. But when they do the happy dance, they're momma's little boy again. They know how to celebrate.

In the book of Esther, at the end of the killing, the following day was a day of feasting and joy. The entire remainder of Chapter 9 consists of the establishment of Purim, a time set aside each year to celebrate God's deliverance. In the early chapters of the book of Esther, the wicked Haman appeared to prosper. But ultimately God's justice prevailed. And it was worth celebrating.

Purim is not a solemn festival. It is joyous; raucous even, in the reenactment of Haman's demise. It is a celebration of the lives of the Jews that were spared. It is a celebration of victory over Haman's evil plan. Purim also celebrates the common bond of all Jewish people—whether in the capital city or in the rural countryside. During Purim, Jews the world over celebrate.

God also triumphed over evil when Jesus became human. When Jesus died for our sins, He overcame death so that we could live forever in God's presence. That is God's great plan for our deliverance. And we should celebrate that deliverance every day of our earthly lives and every day of our eternal lives. God loves it when we celebrate what He has done for us. Need some Scriptural inspiration about God's deliverance?

> *The Lord is my rock, my fortress and my deliverer* (2 Samuel 22:2).

> *call on me in the day of trouble; I will deliver you, and you will honor me* (Psalm 50:15).

> *He lifted me out of the slimy pit, out of the mud and mire; he set my feet on a rock and gave me a firm place to stand* (Psalm 40:2).

> *Everyone who calls on the name of the Lord will be saved* (Romans 10:13).

> *For he has rescued us from the dominion of darkness and brought us into the kingdom of the Son he loves, in whom we have redemption, the forgiveness of sins* (Colossians 1:13-14).

See also Psalm 34:4, Psalm 40:13; Psalm 107:20; Lamentations 3:58-60; Romans 6:14-19.

How about some Scriptural inspiration about celebrating?

> *Praise the LORD. Praise God in his sanctuary; praise him in his mighty heavens. Praise him for his acts of power; praise him for his surpassing greatness.*

> *Praise him with the sounding of the trumpet, praise him with the harp and lyre, praise him with timbrel and dancing, praise him with the strings and pipe, praise him with the clash of cymbals, praise him with resounding cymbals. Let everything that has breath praise the LORD. Praise the LORD* (Psalm 150:1-6).

> *Wearing a linen ephod, David was dancing before the Lord with all his might, while he and all Israel were bringing up the ark of the Lord with shouts and the sound of trumpets* (2 Samuel 6: 14-15).

King David knew how to do a happy dance before God. And he didn't care who saw him do his wild and uncoordinated leaping about. Are we like that? Can we express our all-out, joy-filled celebration of what God has done for us?

Many Bible scholars agree that the book of Esther and specifically the joyful celebration of Purim hints at something greater to come. Purim involved a celebration over an act of deliverance from an enemy, echoing the events of Revelation 19 and reminding us of the joy we have because God has delivered us from spiritual bondage.[9] So much greater will be in celebration of our eternal deliverance by Jesus from an even greater enemy, Satan.

If Esther were here she would say this was her story. She understood the joy of her people's deliverance.

Who are we to God? When we recognize God's plan of deliverance through Jesus and live our lives in celebration, we understand how He might see His women of faith. We can answer:

I am like Esther.

---

[9] Ortlund, *ESV Exhaustive Commentary*, 287.

For Thought and Discussion

- What are some tangible ways to celebrate God's deliverance?

- We acknowledge God's deliverance through Jesus from eternal damnation. In what areas of your life has God *personally* delivered you?

- In the Christian calendar, Christmas and Easter are the holy days that most remind us of God's deliverance—first, Jesus' becoming human and second, Jesus' death and resurrection for our eternal sake. What do these two holy days mean to you?

PRAYER: Heavenly Father, thank you for your deliverance. I know that can you deliver me each day from temptation, when I lean upon your strength. I know that you have delivered me eternally through my trust in Jesus. Please help me keep your deliverance in my hearts and trust in your deliverance as the true promise that it is. And please show me ways to celebrate your deliverance with joy. Amen.

Day 27—I Celebrate Life

~

Celebrate good times! Come On! Cool and the Gang have the right idea. Celebrate good times. I love a good celebration. And believe me when I say that I try to celebrate as often as I can. A birthday? Of course. Cake, ice cream, a special dinner, presents, ribbons, music, dancing, confetti, singing. Anniversaries, graduations, promotions, retirements, goals achieved, Friday nights. Saturday afternoons. National peanut butter sandwich day. There's never a reason too insignificant to celebrate. Never a day when things have gone so badly that they still can't contain something to be grateful for.

One of my favorite Bible verses is Philippians 4:6-7:

> *Do not be anxious about anything, but in every situation, by prayer and petition, with thanksgiving, present your requests to God. And the peace of God, which transcends all understanding, will guard your hearts and your minds in Christ Jesus.*

God took years to instill in my heart the realization that every situation, every crisis, every blessing, ever moment of every day is a reason to be thankful. Every situation, every crisis, every blessing, every moment of every day is worthy of celebration. Even those painful ones. Because God is there with me.

Purim is a joyful celebration. The victory of the Jews over their enemies through Esther happened centuries ago. But today, Jews around the world continue to celebrate the occasion each and every year.

Yesterday we considered how to celebrate God's deliverance of us from the Evil One. Today we take celebration a step further as we realize that every day we live with Christ as our Savior is a day to celebrate our new life *in Him* and our forever, eternal life *with Him*.

The whole of Psalm 118 is filled with praise; in fact most of the entire Book of Psalms is praise. But one of the most beloved and quoted Bible verses is Psalm 118:24, *"Today is the day the LORD has made; let us rejoice and be glad in it."*

Look back through the book of Esther. How many banquets can you count? Esther held two banquets. King Xerxes began the story with a 7-day banquet. Even Queen Vashti hosted one. And don't you think those first 180 days that King Xerxes used to show off his wealth contained a banquet or two? Those Persians knew how to celebrate.

Likewise, the Jews still celebrate Purim each year. Each year becomes a time to remember and celebrate an event that God orchestrated centuries ago. If King Xerxes can host a 7-day banquet; if the Jewish people can celebrate a long ago event, we can certainly raise up a daily prayer of gratitude and live a life of celebration for all that God does in our lives.

If Esther were here she would say this was her story. She encouraged others to celebrate life.

Who are we to God? When we realize the scope of God's love and live in celebration, we understand how God might see His women of faith. We can answer:

I am like Esther.

For Thought and Discussion

- Meditate on this verse today: *Today is the day the Lord has made. I will rejoice and be glad in it* (Psalm 118:24). What thoughts of celebration does it bring to you?

- How does your attitude affect the way you accomplish tasks and meet challenges?

- How can you focus on life as a celebration today?

PRAYER: Heavenly Father, thank you for this day and every day you give me. Please remind me that each day is a gift to be celebrated with gratitude. Help me live with joy and share that joy with people in my lives. Thank you for this life and the life with you to come. Amen.

Day 28—I am Like Esther

❧

And who knows but that you have come to royal position for such a time as this? (Esther 4:14)

When God pointed me to this verse and suggested I write a book about how He sees His women of faith, He and had a little discussion. It went like this:

GOD: Carol, I'd like you to write a book about the lessons women can learn from the book of Esther.

me: Really, God? A whole book about the book of Esther? But you're not even mentioned in it.

GOD: I AM not mentioned; but I AM there. Now, how about writing that book?

me: God, you're aware that the entire book of Esther is only about 20 pages including commentary and footnotes. How about a nice series of blog posts instead?

GOD: Please sit down, daughter and read.

In eventual obedience I began jotting down the lessons we women of faith could learn from the book of Esther. After I had listed lesson number 23, I put down my pencil. I flipped through the remaining six chapters containing lessons I'd not yet discovered and bowed my head in prayer, saying

> *Thank you God for being patient as I struggle in obedience to you. Please remind me in the future of this experience and help me be obedient earlier in the process. And God, thank you for asking me to share your lessons with other women you love.*

Thus, Esther 4:14 became my life verse as I wrote this book. *And who knows but that you have come to royal position for such a time as this?* God has led me through the understanding of ways in which my character and circumstances are similar to those of beautiful Queen Esther.

Because God recorded Queen Esther's life for us in Scripture, we now recognize that we are orphans and exiles, noble not born to royalty, but are adopted daughters of King Jesus as well as His Bride. Our challenge now is:

> *How do we use our status as Ambassadors of the King to go out into the world and live lives that represent Him?*

Because of Queen Esther's teachings, we recognize that we are beautiful and pure in God's sight. We take stewardship over our bodies. We desire to be obedient and seek His guidance in all things. Our challenge now is:

> *How does our understanding of our beauty in God's eyes give us confidence to grab hold of His love and share it more eagerly with others?*

Because of Queen Esther's teachings, we recognize that we can be used by Him wherever and whenever He needs us. We have power through His Spirit, and are steadfast and patient in using that power wisely. Our challenge now is:

> *How does this recognition of God's empowerment push us forward to doing the things He desires us to do in the world?*

Because of Queen Esther's teachings, we recognize that we are stronger when we are part of a community of believers and when we focus on others rather than on ourselves. We recognize our courage through God and live in confidence that we can stand in God's Inner Court and approach His Throne with full assurance of His love. We see our duty in Christ and accept our roles, living them as Christ desires. Our challenge now is:

> *How can our access to God encourage us to a stronger and more personal relationship with Him?*

Because of Queen Esther's teaching, we recognize that we can trust in God's justice and humble ourselves before Him. We can daily celebrate God's abundant blessings and His deliverance from the Evil One. Our challenge now is:

> *How can we live our one and only lives more fully for God, sharing our joy in Him and His desire to bless others and deliver them also from evil?*

I belong to Christ. I'm bought and paid for with His blood. I belong to His family. I'm His child. His daughter. I'm a sister to other Christians. God's kid. Daughter of Abba Father God. That's a mighty fine royal position. And I'd better remember as I go through life that other folks will be watching to see how the King's daughter "does life."

> *And who knows but that you have come to royal position for such a time as this?* (Esther 4:14).

I like my new life verse and its outward focus on others. It is heart evidence of the growth in my faith and trust in Him. I love how God then brought me closer to His throne so He could whisper a secret of love to share with the rest of the world. I am His child. So are you, dear one.

Esther exemplifies how a person can live in the world but not be of the world. This truth was commanded by Jesus (John 15:19; 17:15) and echoed in the New Testament letters (1 John 2:15; Romans 12:2; Colossians 3:2). Although, like Esther, we live today in a world of lavish excesses and social thinking and activities that are not godly, we nonetheless are called to live in the world while not being of this world.

Similarly, we are called to advance God's mission, witnessing our faith (1 Peter 3:15) so as to potentially advance God's mission in other people's lives. That witnessing may be part of the good works God has prepared us to do (Ephesians 2:10) or advance His kingdom in a way we cannot even imagine. But like Esther, we can choose to participate in God's plan—to be used by Him right here and right now.

If Esther were here she would say that this was her story. And she would be glad to share with us what she learned by the life she lived.

With that thought, I further urge you to consider additional, more personal applications as you study the women in the Bible. The theme of this *With Faith Like Hers* series is that our lives, like the women in Scripture, are part of God's ongoing plan. As I was writing this series, my daughter suggested we honor these women in some unique, more personal way. Our business, Her Legacy Beauty[10] was born.

Our business creates beauty products in fragrances that honor biblical women to reflect their unique character or circumstances. Christian women appreciate the reminder of those women's lives in Scripture and find that wearing a unique fragrance is often a conversation starter to talk about Jesus. "Oh, you smell so good," your friend might say. You respond with, "Let me tell you about the woman whose fragrance I'm wearing and her place in the Bible." Your friend has just opened a conversation to talk about Jesus.

This example is not about me peddling my company. This is about me encouraging you to find a way to incorporate your understanding of these women in the Bible into your daily life. Study the women. Consider how their character and circumstances are similar to your own. Then do something with that understanding. You might be surprised where it leads. I was.

Dear sister, I pray that you and I will continue to learn the lessons Queen Esther teaches God's women of faith. I pray that you and I will grow stronger in our faith in Jesus. One day—when we meet in heaven—we won't need name tags to recognize each other. You'll know my name and I'll know yours. God Himself will call us by name. It might be the name we've been known by here on Earth. Or it might be that name we share because it's how He sees His women of faith.

Until then...

Love, Esther

---

[10] www.HerLegacyBeauty.com.

For Thought and Discussion

- In what ways did you end this study feeling like Esther?

- In what ways do you feel you need to grow into becoming more like Esther?

- What steps will you take now to live as the woman of faith God desires you to be?

PRAYER: Heavenly Father, thank you for your Word and for the lives of people recorded in it. Thank you for their examples that help us know how you want us to live a life that reflects your glory to the world. Please help me become the woman of faith you desire. Help me learn the lessons Esther can teach me. Help me live a life of faithfulness to you. Amen.

Celebrating Purim

The Jewish festival of Purim is generally celebrated in late winter or early spring. The exact date is based on the ancient Jewish calendar. Because the Jewish calendar is different from our 365-day solar-based calendar, the date for Purim each year changes. Most recently, the festival takes place in March. The name of the festival—Purim—gets its name from the Jewish word *pur. Pur* means "lot" (as in dice) and refers to the fact that the date Haman chose for the annihilation of the Jews was selected by tossing the *pur* (rolling the dice).

The Scroll of Esther (our book of Esther), referred to as the *megillah* is read aloud in Jewish synagogues at the beginning of Purim. Folks "boo," stomp their feet, and use noisemakers when Haman's name comes up. The events are often re-enacted and children typically dress up as various characters from the story. Gifts, money given to charity, and celebratory dinners are common.

A traditional Purim treat are Hamantaschen. These cookies are named after evil Haman. They are filled with jam and made in tri-angular shapes, to represent evil Haman's tri-cornered Persian hat. On the next page is a recipe for you to try yourself. If you find it difficult to keep the pinched corners together during baking (many people do; me included), simply fold the circles in half to form a semi-circle and tell folks his hat, like evil Haman himself, was defeated.

Most importantly, enjoy. And celebrate your deliverance by Jesus!

Purim Hamantaschen Cookies

(Makes about 2 dozen cookies)

8 ounces butter, softened
8 ounces cream cheese, softened
1/4 cup sugar
1 teaspoon vanilla
2 cups flour plus 1/8 cup flour
Strawberry or apricot jam
Powdered sugar for garnish

Cream together the butter, cheese, sugar and vanilla. Work in the flour and chill for at least one hour. On a floured surface, roll the dough to about 1/4 inch thick. Cut 4 inch circles using a glass dipped in flour or round cookie cutter.

Place each circle onto an ungreased cookie sheet. Spoon a scant 1 teaspoon of jam into the center and pinch the edges to create three corners with filling showing. (Or just fold over into a semi-circle and press edges together to seal in the jam.)

Bake at 350 for 20-25 minutes until golden. Sprinkle with powdered sugar when cool.

Resources

The following are a few of the resources used in preparation of this book. Each of the scholarly resources also have their own extensive bibliographies. If you want to dig deeper, you can work your way through those bibliographies.

Baker, Warren and Eugene Carpenter, eds. *Complete Word Study Dictionary Old Testament*. Chattanooga, TN: AMG, 2003.

Baker, Warren, Tim Rake, and David Kemp. *Complete Word Study Old Testament, King James Version*. Chattanooga, TN: AMG, 1994.

These two volumes work together as a single resource for Old Testament Hebrew words and phrases. When researching a specific word or phrase, first go to the *Old Testament* volume and find the specific word in that passage of Scripture. Above that word will be a code. That code is then used to locate exactly how that original word in Hebrew was used—it's meaning and intention *in that specific verse of Scripture* in the second volume. See the companion 2-volume set for the New Testament listed below.

Benner, Drayton, *ESV Exhaustive Concordance*. Wheaton, IL: Crossway,. 2018.

As its title describes, this concordance is "exhaustive." It lists passages according to specific words they contain. For example, taking the word "fear," this concordance then lists almost 400 verses that use that word (there are additional listings for "feared," fearful," "fearfully," "fearing," "fears" and "fearsome"). This resource can be helpful when researching specific topics.

Biblegateway.com.

This is a fabulous online resource. It provides a quick and easy way to read the same Scripture in various versions for deeper understanding. It also has quite good commentaries that encourage a desire to find out more.

Buttrick, George Arthur, Commentary Editor. *Interpreter's Bible; The Holy Scriptures in the King James and Revised Standard Versions with General Articles and Introduction, Exegesis, Exposition for Each Book of the Bible.* Volume III. New York: Abingdon Press, 1952.

This 12-volume Bible belonged to my Pastor dad who purchased them during or shortly after seminary. He used them for 45 years of sermon preparation. Now they're my first go-to when I need solid, theological commentary or explanation. This important scholarly resource continues to be published, the latest edition as of the printing of this book was released by Abingdon Press in 2015.

Butterick, George A., *The Interpreter's Dictionary of the Bible, An Illustrated Encyclopedia.* New York: Abingdon Press, 1962.

This four-volume resource is valuable for understanding people and places discussed in the Bible. It includes archaeological discoveries as well as research into the life of people in ancient times.

Calef, Susan and Ronald A. Simkins, ed., "Women, Gender, and Religion," *Journal of Religion & Society,* The Kripke Center: 2009, Supplement Series 5, p. 155-169.

This journal article was especially helpful in providing background for the book of Esther and Queen Vashti in particular.

Comfort, Philip W. and Walter A. Elwell, eds. *Tyndale Bible Dictionary.* Carol Stream, IL: Tyndale, 2001.

This is an excellent resource to start a research on individual words, phrases, and theological concepts.

Deen, Edith, *All of the Women of the Bible.* San Francisco: Harper San Francisco, 1983.

This book gives a general overview of women in Scripture. It is easy to read without being scholarly.

Elwell, Walter A. *Theological Dictionary.* Grand Rapids, MI: Baker Book House, 1989.

This resource and the one below are two different theological dictionaries. While there is some overlap, both are good resources to begin an understanding on words, phrases, and theological concepts.

Elwell, Walter A., *Evangelical Dictionary of Theology.* Grand Rapids, MI: Baker Academic, 2001.

Like the one above, this is another excellent resource to start a research on individual words, phrases, and theological concepts.

Green, Jay. P, Sr., *The Interlinear Bible Hebrew-Greek-English,* Peabody, MS: Hendrickson Publishers. 1986.

This is a single volume of the Bible with each word of text containing the Hebrew or Greek word used in the original. Each word is tied to the Strong's Concordance number for cross-referencing. This, like the Baker and Zodhiates resources help better interpret Scripture in a word-by-word format.

Hamilton, Victor P., *Handbook on the Historical Books.* Grand Rapids, MI: Baker Academic, 2001.

This 557-page textbook, covering only the books of Joshua, Judges, Ruth, Samuel, Kings, Chronicles, Ezra-Nehemiah, and Esther was mandatory reading in seminary. It contains an exhaustive bibliography the author used to research the book of Esther. It was most helpful understanding the historical aspects of Esther, the Persian empire, and biblical interpretation of the book.

Megillah. Various publishers are available.

The *megillah* is Hebrew for scroll. There are five *megillahs,* all of which are also included in the Christian Bible. They are Song of Songs, Ruth, Lamentations, Ecclesiastes, and Esther. Esther is traditionally read each year at the time of Purim aloud at the synagogue, often from a handwritten parchment scroll. For our purposes, we Christians typically read from the book of Esther in our Christian Bible. You can, however, find many versions of the Jewish *Megillah* with English translation and commentary.

Midrash Rabbah

There are two types of midrash—*aggadic* (narrative) and *halakhic* (legal). Esther, part of the five Megillot, is part of the *aggadic midrash.* This collection is referred to as *Midrash Rabbah,* which Jewish tradition indicates refers to a name: Rabbi Oshaya Rabbah, the first rabbi quoted in that midrash.

MyJewishLearning.com. accessed 3/17/25.

While not a scholarly site, this resource generally explains Hebrew terms and traditions simply and in a way that could be easily understood, particularly as it relates to explanation of *midrash*.

New Strong's Concise Concordance of the Bible. Nashville, TN: Thomas Nelson, 2005.

This resource is helpful to understand meaning of original words in Scripture and locating passages.

OpenBible.info

This is another good online resource with an ability to search based on a word or topic. Although the results sometimes feel computer generated (because they are!) it's still a good place to start expanding a line of thinking.

Ortlund, Eric, *ESV Expository Commentary, Vol. IV Ezra-Job*, Duguid, Ian M., James M. Hamilton Jr., Jay Sklar. Wheaton, IL: Crossway, 2020.

This multi-volume resource is based on the English Standard Version (ESV) of the Bible. It contains both expository (explanation) and commentary (interpretation) of the book of Esther which augments that of the *Interpreter's Bible* listed above.

Vine, W.E. *Vine's Complete Expository Dictionary of Old and New Testament Words.* Nashville, TN: Thomas Nelson Publishers, 1996.

This Bible dictionary is helpful in understanding the meaning of the original words in Scripture.

Zondervan NIV Study Bible. Grand Rapids: Zondervan, 2002.

This provides basic study notes for a quick overview of Scripture.

Zodhiates, Spiros, Warren Baker, George Hadjiantoniou, and Mark Oshman, eds. *Complete Word Study Dictionary New Testament*. Chattanooga: AMG, 1993.

Zodhiates, Spiros, ThD, Warren Baker, DRE, and Rev. George Hadjiantoniou, PhD, eds. *Complete Word Study Old Testament, King James Version*. Chattanooga: AMG, 1992.

These two volumes work together as a single resource for New Testament Greek words and phrases. When researching a specific word or phrase, first go to the *New Testament* volume and find the specific word. Above that word will be a code. That code is then used to locate exactly how that original word in Hebrew was used—it's meaning and intention *in that specific verse of Scripture.* See the companion 2-volume set for the Old Testament listed above.

Zucker, D. J. (2024). "Viewing Vashti: as Victim, as Vilified, and as Venerated." *Women in Judaism: A Multidisciplinary E-Journal, 20*(1), 1–16.

This resource specifically addressed the question of who Vashti was in history.

The best and most valuable source always—is prayer, study and God's leading. It's easy and tempting to come up with personal theology and proclaim it brilliant. It's harder, but always best, to rely on God's leading and to check any "personal brilliance" against the truth of God's Word set forth in Scripture.

From the Author

I was raised in a Christian home—the daughter of a Protestant minister. But it wasn't until I was in my late twenties that I took full ownership of my faith and began the long process of learning what it means to be a Christian and a child of God. I'm still learning.

When I began writing for publication, I was blessed by early publishing success when my first four books were picked up by a respected children's educational publisher. My mission became to write in a way that would educate, inspire, and entertain others.

Gradually I moved from writing for children to writing for women seeking to deepen their faith in Christ. Someone in the writing world once said that "all writing is basically autobiographical." That's true for me as I write this Bible study series. I seek to understand and deepen my own faith as I write to help other women understand and deepen theirs.

I live in Idaho with my husband of almost 50 years. I have two grown children and two grandsons, who taught me that if God only loves me a fraction of how much I love them—wow, God loves me a lot!

This book is part of a series of Bible studies/Daily Devotionals about selected women of the Bible. To find other books in this series, please go to Amazon.com. You can search for the series by typing in *With Faith Like Hers* followed by *I am*. Each title in the series will begin with "I am" followed by the name of that women.

If you enjoyed this study, please let others know. One of the best ways to let folks know is to leave a review. Just go to Amazon.com, find the title of this book and click on "Write a Customer Review." Thanks in advance!

www.ingramcontent.com/pod-product-compliance
Lightning Source LLC
Chambersburg PA
CBHW072018060426
42446CB00044B/2798

* 9 7 8 1 9 5 1 5 8 7 1 0 9 *